Ancient Olympic Philosophy

Ancient Olympic Philosophy:

Sport
Athletes
Excellence
Women
Beauty
Fairness
Peace

Heather L. Reid

Parnassos Press
2024

First Printing: 2024
ISBN: 978-1-942495-765 (hardcover)
ISBN: 978-1-942495-758 (paperback)
ISBN: 978-1-942495-772 (ebook)

Parnassos Press
Fonte Aretusa Organization
Siracusa, Sicily and Dakota Dunes, SD

www.fontearetusa.org

On the cover: Terracotta statuette of the Diadoumenos, copy of a Greek bronze statue of ca. 430 B.C. by Polykleitos 1st century BCE. Metropolitan Museum of Art Accession Number: 32.11.2. Open Access Image.

Acknowledgments

This book is dedicated to Ancient Olympia and the people who keep its spirit alive, especially Apostolos Kosmopoulos, the Spilopoulos family, and the staff of the International Olympic Academy.

Special thanks for their help and inspiration go to Rafael Mendoza, Larry Theobald, Georgios Mouratidis, Stephen G. Miller, Gregory Nagy, Charles H. Stocking, Stamatia Dova, the Harvard Center for Hellenic Studies, and all the other students and colleagues with whom I have and continue to seek knowledge in Olympia.

About the Author

Heather L. Reid is Scholar in Residence at the Exedra Mediterranean Center in Siracusa, Sicily, and Professor of Philosophy Emerita at Morningside College in Sioux City, Iowa. She is a 2015 Fellow of the American Academy in Rome, 2018-2020 Fellow of Harvard's Center for Hellenic Studies in Washington DC, and 2019 Fulbright Scholar at the Università degli Studi di Napoli Federico II. A competitive cyclist in her youth, she was a national intercollegiate champion on both the track and road and a medalist in the California State Games. She has authored numerous books and articles in ancient philosophy, philosophy of sport, and Olympic Studies, and has lectured on these topics in Beijing, London, Rome, Seoul, and at the International Olympic Academy in Olympia, Greece.

Table of Contents

Entrance to the stadium at Ancient Olympia
photo: author

Introduction

To enter Olympia's ancient stadium is a special feeling even today. Walking through the remains of the tunnel that connects the sanctuary and sporting ground, it is hard not to wonder how the ancient athletes felt. After all, most of us have competed in sports and we know the feelings of uncertainty and hope that every athlete—ancient or modern—faces at the start of an event. Most of us have experienced modern stadiums filled with spectators, maybe even Olympic stadiums, and we can easily imagine the grassy slopes in Olympia teeming with enthusiastic fans.

Making your way onto the track, you might stand on the ancient stone starting block. Maybe you even remove your shoes and socks to curl your naked toes into the same beveled groove from which ancient Olympic champions started their races. Probably you know that they ran completely naked, their oiled skin glistening in the sun. Looking down, you see the square holes that held the ancient starting gate, looking up you see a marble altar to the left and a section of stone seats off to the right. You may know that the priestess of Demeter Chamyne observed the Games from that altar and that the stone seats held officials called *Hellanodikai*.

Still, you can't help but wonder as you stand on that ancient starting block, what did all of this *mean* to the ancient Greeks? How did their Olympic Games differ from ours? How were they similar? What was the purpose of sport for them? How did they think about athletes? Why did they compete in the nude? Did women ever race on this track? What did those beautiful athletic statues symbolize? What did the judges consider to be fair? How did this place and its Games come to represent an ideal of peace?

These questions are historical but also philosophical, and Ancient Greece offers a great philosophical tradition with which to explore them. Olympia is as much a place of ideas as it is a place of sport, and I have spent most of my scholarly career trying to understand these ideas. This book is designed to explain ancient Olympic philosophy to non-specialists who are nevertheless curious about the links between ancient and modern sport.

The essays are organized according to the themes of sport, athletes, excellence, women, beauty, fairness, and peace. All are based on articles published in academic journals, but each has been revised for easy reading with most of the scholarly apparatus and professional jargon removed. I have also added some helpful images, a glossary of ancient Greek terms, and a bibliography that lists not only the ancient and modern sources referenced but also works recommended for further reading.

The Olympic Games are built upon more than sport; their foundations include philosophical ideals from Ancient Greece and prehistoric religious rituals. At the same time, sport itself contains a philosophy that cannot be separated from Ancient Olympia and its history. My hope is that these essays will help people to better appreciate Ancient Olympia, the Olympic Games, and sport itself. Everyone who plays a sport or thinks philosophically anywhere in the world owes something to Ancient Olympia.

Siracusa, Sicily
December 2024

Original Scholarly Articles

The chapters in this book derive from articles published in scholarly journals. Those seeking the more detailed notes and bibliography should consult these originals:

Sport: Heather L. Reid, "Sport, Philosophy, and the Quest for Knowledge," *Journal of the Philosophy of Sport* 36.1 (2009): 40-49, DOI: 10.1080/00948705.2009.9714744. Reprinted by permission of Informa UK Limited, Taylor & Francis Group.

Athletes: Heather L. Reid, "Olympic Heroes: The Ion P. Ioannides Lecture 2021," *Olympika: The International Journal of Olympic Studies* 30 (2021): 22-39. Reprinted by permission.

Excellence: Heather Reid and Georgios Mouratidis, "Naked Virtue: Ancient Athletic Nudity and the Olympic Ethos of *Aretē*," *Olympika: The International Journal of Olympic Studies* 29 (2020): 29-55. Reprinted by permission.

Women: Heather Reid, "Women and Ancient Olympic Ideals: A Closer Look," *Olympika: The International Journal of Olympic Studies* 32 (2023): 88-101. Reprinted by permission.

Beauty: Heather Reid, "Athletic Virtue and Aesthetic Values in Aristotle's Ethics," *Journal of the Philosophy of Sport* 47.1 (2020) 63-74, DOI10.1080/00948705.2019.1691923. Reprinted by permission of Informa UK Ltd, Taylor & Francis Group.

Fairness: Heather L. Reid, "Aristotle on the Beauty of Fair Play," *Estetica: Studi e Ricerche,* 11.1 (2021): 201-10. Reprinted by permission.

Peace: Heather L. Reid, "Olympic Sport and Its Lessons for Peace," *Journal of the Philosophy of Sport* 33.2 (2006): 205-14, DOI: 10.1080/00948705.2006.9714702. Reprinted by permission of Informa UK Limited, Taylor & Francis Group.

Terracotta Panathenaic prize amphora
Attributed to the Euphiletos painter, ca. 530 BCE. Metropolitan
Museum of Art. Number: 14.130.1232.11.2. Open Access Image.

Sport:

Olympic Sport and the Quest for Knowledge

Sport in Ancient Olympia was serious business. This is not to say that it served commercial ends, much less the recreational or entertainment aims that it does today. Ancient Olympic sport was rather a knowledge-seeking activity that served religious, social, and educational goals. It was serious business because it provided a way of seeking truth independent from social hierarchies and cultural traditions. Similar to philosophy, democracy, lawcourts, and other forms of competitive truth seeking that emerged in ancient Greece, Olympic-style athletic contests display the characteristics of (a) authentic questioning, (b) impartial testing, and (c) public demonstration of results; features that endure in modern science.

Olympic sport was born with these knowledge-seeking characteristics, not least because it was conceived in response to an emerging philosophical recognition of the fallibility of humanity and its traditional hierarchies. By setting up rational, impartial, and publicly observed selection methods, both Olympic-style sport and philosophical inquiry managed to subvert worldly power and authority in a way that fostered agreement among diverse communities without suppressing personal individuality.

Sport and philosophy were eventually adapted to the educational function of cultivating individual *aretē* (excellence, virtue) or, in modern parlance, moral character. As we continue to pursue social and educational goals through sport, it is important to understand how these functions were related in ancient times to the philosophical characteristics of Olympic sport. Indeed we may better put sport in the service of humanity today by viewing it not merely as a playful pastime, but also as a philosophical activity—as an expression of what

1

Aristotle described in the opening of his *Metaphysics* as the natural and universal human desire to learn and know.

Truth-Seeking through Sport

In his eighth Olympian ode, Pindar, the ancient Greek poet famed for his praise of victorious athletes, praises the sanctuary at Olympia for its knowledge-seeking character:

> *O mother of the golden-crowned games,*
> *Olympia, mistress of truth, where men who are seers*
> *examine burnt offerings and test*
> *Zeus of the bright thunderbolt,*
> *to see if he has any word concerning mortals*
> *who are striving in their hearts*
> *to gain a great success*
> *and respite from their toils;*

The association between Olympia and knowledge seeking derives partly from the existence of an oracle at the site, but also from the less tangible sentiment that athletic results from Olympia were reliable indicators of truth about the gods' wishes and the relative merits of athletes and their tribes.

There was nothing new or revolutionary in the association between athletics and truth. Our earliest accounts of sport-like activities (up to a millennium before the Olympic Games) among Mesopotamians, Egyptians, Assyrians, Minoans, and Hittites show royals using athletic display as public evidence for social standing and worthiness to lead. Rarely, if ever, was the worthiness of the ruler actually challenged, however. What was distinctive about Hellenic athletics and Olympic-style contests was precisely that they were knowledge-seeking, rather than presumption-affirming because their outcomes were uncertain, they were governed by impartial rules, and they were subject to public scrutiny.

As a result, Olympic sport was subversive from its start. But what it subverted were dogmatic and relativistic standards for truth (i.e., those controlled by worldly rank and power), and what it promoted were more impartial and universal standards, the kind capable of settling disagreements among diverse and even warring tribes.

Philosophical inquiry emerged later in the 6th century BCE as an approach to studying nature with similar characteristics and similar results. Having encountered competing religious and mythological claims from neighboring cultures, the Presocratic philosophers sought a more impartial and demonstrable method of understanding nature—one that bypassed worldly authority and social hierarchies.

Sport has the power to challenge social hierarchies, as it always has, but it faces resistance, as it always has, from those whose power it challenges. To preserve Olympic sport's truth-seeking function we must appreciate its link with authentic questioning, impartial testing, and public display of evidence.

Uncertainty and Authentic Questioning

The Greek term *philosophia,* which literally means "love of wisdom," seems to have been coined in the 6th century BCE by Pythagoras, who used it to describe those rare thinkers, like himself, who acknowledged not their wisdom but rather their ignorance. It was of course Socrates who made this conception of philosophy famous by declaring more than a century later that his renowned "wisdom" derived precisely from his awareness that he lacked knowledge.

We cannot truly love and desire what we think we already possess; so we are philosophers only as long as we pursue authentic questions with uncertain answers. Sport, likewise, is philosophical only as long as it is actually open to finding answers that may conflict with what people already believe. Olympic contests should not be designed to affirm the status quo or any other predetermined outcome: they should reflect the spirit of really wanting to know.

Ancient Egypt provides a negative example: when challengers boxed the pharaoh, the question of who would win was not authentic and its answer was not uncertain because the pharaoh always won. Though such contests were supposed to convince subjects of their pharaoh's divine invincibility, they begged their own question—what does a contest prove if its winner is chosen ahead of time? True Olympic sport, like philosophy and all effective forms of knowledge-seeking, begins with authentic questions derived from real uncertainty.

Where did such "authentic questions" come from? What prompted Presocratic philosophy and sport as described in Homer and practiced at Olympia to embrace the uncertain, impartial, and public pursuit of truth? The answer is simple: competing claims among divergent stakeholders. Mycenean funeral games, perhaps the earliest form of knowledge-seeking sport, settled competing claims to the deceased's property. The funeral games depicted in Homer's *Iliad* take this concept even further by also negotiating Achilles' and Agamemnon's competing claims to honor and authority.

At Olympia, Philostratus tells us in *Gymnasticus* 5 that the religious puzzle of who should have the honor of lighting the sacrificial flame came to be solved by a footrace from the edge of the sanctuary to the altar. Meanwhile in 6th century BCE Ionia, increased contact among diverse cultures in the absence of overarching authority prompted the development of a more universal method of truth-seeking. It shouldn't be a surprise that the method they invented (now known as philosophy and early natural science) resembled athletic games, since both practices were responses to competing truth-claims.

What was distinctive (and subversive) about the Olympic and philosophical methods of truth-seeking is that the answering of the questions is delegated to the contest rather than tradition or authority. In this way, they exhibit the characteristically philosophical quality of uncertainty or acknowledged ignorance. Although modern sport no longer addresses questions about religious favor or worthiness to lead, it still negotiates competing claims to excellence and often decides the distribution of valuable rewards including educational opportunities. It is important, therefore, to remain sensitive to the authenticity of the process by keeping social presumptions from compromising the integrity of the contest.

The athletic success of marginalized groups certainly has helped to subvert modern social hierarchies, and it is widely recognized that preemptive exclusion of participants based on social categories runs counter to the logic of philosophical contest. But *de-facto* exclusion based on sex and inequities derived from financial disparity persist in sport, drawing little criticism, perhaps because they reflect our presumptions about athletic excellence. Sport's ability to subvert social hierarchies requires first that we honor its philosophical heritage of authentic questioning.

Open and Impartial Testing

The very act of authentic questioning displays intellectual humility with respect to truth, but for sport to be philosophical, humility must also apply to the construction of the test. If your method for resolving disputes is to let local authorities decide, or even to set armies to battle, you haven't fully acknowledged the limitations of the human mind. Insofar as "truth" is understood as something universal and eternal, knowledge of such truths must be reliable and demonstrable; not just a matter of belief, persuasion, or worldly power (military, political, or otherwise).

The ancient Greek philosopher Heraclitus famously said that you cannot step into the same river twice, revealing that the world we perceive is constantly in flux. If we want to know something universal, we must approach it through reason. This is why the followers of Pythagoras sought to understand the *kosmos* (universe) using impartial criteria such as number and proportion.

It is also why Olympia's judges and organizers (the so-called *Hellanodikai*) enforced the rules strictly and rejected all subjectively judged events. Since their goal was to dedicate truly excellent victors to a supremely wise god, their own biases and preferences couldn't be allowed to interfere. Impartial mechanisms for truth-seeking act to neutralize the effects of human fallibility and worldly bias, providing equal opportunity for diverse possibilities: athletes as well as ideas.

The basic features of Olympic sport such as common starting lines and level playing fields exhibit the philosophical drive for rational impartiality. Already in Homer's Bronze Age, the fair construction of contests is emphasized. In the chariot race, for example, there is no permanent track, so a common starting line is literally drawn in the sand and the reliable elder Phoenix is sent off to referee the turnaround point. The starting positions are determined by drawing lots, and when young Antilochos recklessly cuts off Menelaos at a narrow stream crossing, a dispute erupts over the validity of the results. A serious discussion and redistribution of prizes ensues until the community is satisfied with the end result.

The Homeric creed "to always be the best and outdo others" generated authentic questions about who was indeed best. In the context of hand-to-hand combat, the demonstration of a warrior's *aretē* is important, and contests provided a relatively impartial mechanism not just to affirm, but to impartially test it. Insofar as the community's welfare depends on contest results, it is essential to Olympic sport's social and philosophical functions that contests be constructed and conducted impartially.

Modern sports rules generally respect the principles of impartial testing; competitors even switch sides in field and court games just in case it provides some advantage. On the other hand, the competitive and often greedy drive to gain every possible advantage sets up an antagonistic relationship between competitors and officials that often leaves the purpose of the contest behind. Just as with scientific experiments, the value of the results depends on the integrity of the test.

This means not only that competitors must obey contest rules, but officials must also carefully enforce them. To be sure, different individuals are free to pursue a variety of personal interests though sport. But the goods that all of us seek— results, revenue, honor, entertainment—ultimately depend for their value upon the integrity and impartiality of the contest.

Public Display of Evidence

The third characteristic of philosophical sport is public observation of the contest and the effect this has on acceptance of the results. Rooting for one's favorite athlete or team is as much a part of sports as arguing for one's thesis is part of philosophical inquiry. In neither practice, however, should the winner be determined by who supports it or even how many support it. Rather, each candidate should be subjected to the rational and impartial test before everyone's eyes. The public's interest in accurate results requires that popular opinion defer to demonstrable evidence.

Open demonstration also motivates acceptance of contest results by fostering consensus without appeal to tradition, authority, faith, or violence. Indeed the unifying and pacifying effects of athletic games were thought to contribute to Hellenic unity. A sacred truce called *ekecheiria* made the Olympic Games a rare opportunity for diverse (and often warring) tribes to come together for the common cause of worship. Intellectuals came to exchange ideas just as boxers came to exchange blows. Indeed, intertribal contact at Olympia fostered economic trade as well as the political negotiation of peace.

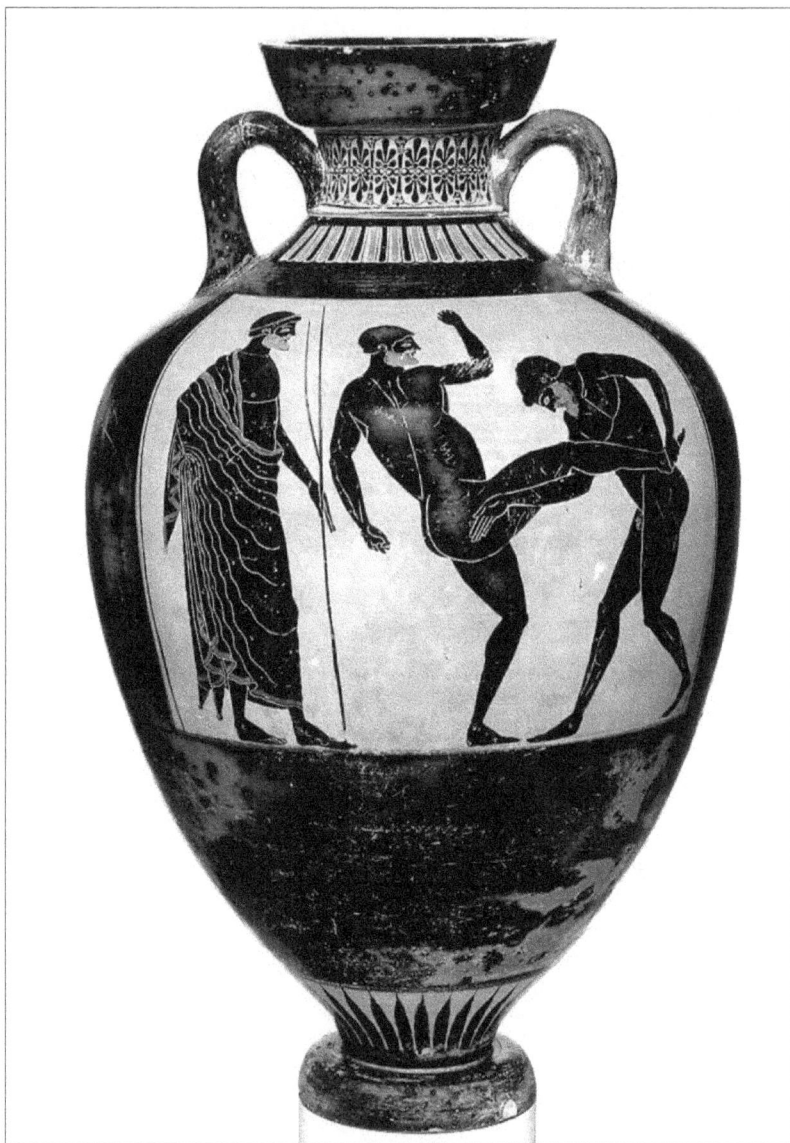

Terracotta Panathenaic prize amphora, ca. 500 BCE.
An official keeps order during a combat event.
Metropolitan Museum of Art number 16.71. Open access image.

Getting rivals to agree on anything—even to imagine that they could agree—takes more than a safe time and place, however. It takes common interest in a common cause. Since the worshippers at Olympia had a common interest in selecting victors who would please the relevant god, they took a common interest in the validity of contest results. For this reason, nothing was left to chance. A month-long pre-Olympic training camp was held at the nearby city of Elis to assure the worthiness of every candidate. At the Games competitors were literally stripped of cultural differences and outward signs of social inequality, and a stadium was built so that everyone could observe the competitive process.

No doubt political rivalries played out in the Games, and among the spectators. But the fact of public scrutiny facilitated acceptance of the results even when they subverted personal preference or conventional wisdom. Most important, the cooperation dramatized in sport paved the way for economic and military cooperation without subjection to a single authority. Through the use of such mechanisms as blind review and public presentation, philosophers and scientists engage in a similar kind of competitive cooperation for the common cause of truth, one ideally independent of power, politics, cultural ideology.

Modern sport is still subject to widespread public scrutiny, albeit increasingly through telecommunications and digital media. Modern Olympic athletes are scrutinized in slow-motion and from every possible angle. This process serves to increase public confidence in the results. Once a sport loses public credibility, however, its potential for social subversion dries up. Both the impartiality of the test and the authenticity of the question are drawn into doubt, and we regress to the pharaoh's boxing match with dispassionate and incredulous spectators. Modern sport remains a worthy way to challenge social hierarchies and assumptions, but only as long as we value and preserve its ancient philosophical structure.

Education through Sport

The knowledge-seeking character of competitive sport in ancient Greece may explain why "gymnastics" in the form of athletic training and intramural competition became an integral part of moral education. Confusion abounded even in Plato's day about how exercises apparently focused on bodily health could build the moral strength we now call "character." Likely it was the youth's obsession with sports and athletic training that first led Socrates into Athens' gymnasia where he learned and adapted tricks from the athletes' trade to turn young men's souls away from the love of victory (*philonikia*) and toward the love of wisdom (*philosophia*).

But this educational journey, at least for Plato, does not leave athletics behind. Rather, the force of character revealed and developed through sport seems essential for those who would become philosopher-kings in the ideal city he describes in the *Republic*. This is because intentional movement of the body (*sōma*) was thought to be an expression of the mind/soul (*psychē*). The fit athletic body was accordingly understood as a product of personal effort and self-discipline that served as a testament to the *aretē* of the soul. Its beauty was associated with moral goodness and intentionally cultivated in gymnasia.

Socratic Contest

It is well known that Socrates turned earlier philosophers' investigations of the natural world toward the explicitly educational ends of moral philosophy. Less well known are the connections between the Socratic method known as *elenchos* and athletic contest. Plato's Socratic dialogues exhibit the same characteristics of truth seeking as athletic contests. Like sport, Socratic *elenchos* exposes imperfections, tests for improvement, and provides public evidence of progress.

Socrates was put on trial in 399 BCE for corrupting the youth by publicly exposing local wise men's ignorance. The social subversion already associated with Olympic sport was certainly part of his aim. Indeed he describes his "labors" in Plato's *Apology* as *"ponoi,"* a term associated with the quintessential Olympic hero Heracles, who liberated the Greeks from onerous monsters and tyrants. But Socrates' shame game (the verb for Socratic examination, *elenchō*, can means to examine or put to shame) has the explicitly educational function of motivating personal inquiry.

Just as athletes are motivated by losing (or at least the risk of losing) to spend long hours in training and preparation, Socrates' disclosure of ignorance is designed to motivate serious philosophical inquiry. In this sense it is a benefit, and he describes it in the *Apology* as a service to both the city and to the god, adding that the city should reward him like an Olympic victor, since champions only make the city *think* itself happier, whereas Socrates offers them a chance at true happiness.

This idea that agonistic struggle (with its shaming and defeat) is educational remains central to the presence of sport in schools today. Socrates' use of dialectic clearly aims at the improvement of the individual. "You love to win, Socrates," says Callicles in *Gorgias* 515b; it is a charge the philosopher does not deny. But unlike his rival educators, Socrates is less interested in winning the argument than he is in *winning over* his audience to the practice of philosophy. He exemplifies the friendship aspect of competition, comparing the way he challenges students to a stone that tests gold(486c)—something that brings out the best within them

Socrates' *elenchos* is also described as an intellectual undressing comparable to athletic nudity and aimed explicitly at improvement of the *psychē*. He insists that everyone participate in his contests and chastises the aged Theodorus for

11

refusing to enter the philosophical conversation in Plato's dialogue *Theaetetus* by comparing him to a voyeur at a Spartan wrestling school. Replies Theodorus:

> The Spartans tell one either to strip or to go away; but you seem rather to be playing the part of Antaeus. You don't let any comer go till you have stripped him and made him wrestle with you in the argument.

Socrates' response is telling:

> That, Theodorus, is an excellent simile to describe what is the matter with me. But I am more of a fiend for exercise than Sciron and Antaeus. I have met with many and many a Heracles and Theseus in my time, mighty men of words; and they have well battered me. But for all that I don't retire from the field, so terrible a lust has come upon me for these exercises. You must not begrudge me this, either, try a fall with me and we shall both be the better. (*Theaetetus* 169bc)

Importantly, and unlike today's scholastic sports, submission of oneself to the contest is required—but all contestants are expected to benefit, not just the winners.

Philosophers value the challenge and even refutation of our arguments. Why is public discourse about the value of failure in sports so rare? Misapprehension of athletic goals— even in educational settings—explains this. Sports in schools and Olympic Games alike tend to emphasize victory, but the educational value of public risking is much greater.

Sport in Plato's *Republic*

In Plato's *Republic*, athletics are woven into education explicitly for the purpose of developing souls capable of philosophy and, eventually, community leadership. The authentic question addressed by athletics in this context comes from uncertainty about who should lead. And the role athletics plays in answering that question is not simply the testing of hypotheses, but the testing and selection of souls that can withstand the rigors of mathematical and philosophical education aimed at understanding the Good. Plato also expects athletic soul training to turn individuals' interests away from personal pleasure and material wealth in favor of public service. Indeed the *Republic*'s guardians and philosopher kings do not have personal property or individual families.

The *aretē* sought in Plato's *Republic* is described as the harmonious organization of the intellectual, spirited, and appetitive parts of the *psychē*. Plato seems to think that athletics can achieve this because they require the intellect to apprehend the rules of the game and then to recruit the spirit and appetite to its cause. In another dialogue, *Phaedrus*, this virtuous harmony is illustrated by the athletic metaphor of a two-horse chariot in which the intellect drives a noble and spirited horse alongside the strong but less obedient appetitive horse.

Since athletic success depends on the taming of selfish appetites and the directing of honor or spirit toward the noble ends apprehended by the intellect, sport is thought to train the soul for higher education and ultimately public service. Significantly, Plato doesn't neglect any element of the soul in his account. Appetite and spirit as well as reason are needed to climb the arduous path from the "cave" of mere appearance to the divine light of truth—and the soul can prepare for this educational expedition through athletic training.

Athletics in the *Republic* are not playful. Plato uses them explicitly to train souls and select a social elite who will go on to distinguish themselves in academics and, ultimately, public service. Candidates are to be kept "under observation from childhood," and subjected to "labors, pains, and contests' so that they may be tested "more thoroughly than gold is tested by fire" (413de). Our modern idea that sports are a means to recreation, entertainment, or financial ends are all negated in

Republic by resistance to appetitive desires (for wealth as well as physical pleasure) in the properly ordered soul.

Modern sports, by contrast, are often pursued for profit and at the expense of study and service. Whereas the primacy of wealth is unquestioned today, in Plato's *Republic* the most prestigious careers are based on public service and require the abandonment of personal ambitions as well as one's family and property. As seriously as sports are taken today, I suspect Plato would lament that we don't take them seriously enough to put them explicitly and intentionally in the service of our most important social functions.

Conclusion

Some say that we should look to Rome rather than Greece to see our own athletic values reflected in antiquity. There, they say, sports functioned primarily as entertainment enjoyed by masses of inactive spectators and exploited by politicians who sought public favor. But even the bloody spectacle of gladiator fights preserved the truth-seeking and educational functions that connect sport and philosophy. While the Emperor saluted the Roman spectators, who were seated in tiers according to social class, the contest itself challenged that hierarchy. It gave "socially-dead" gladiators the opportunity to prove their social worth by prevailing in a publicly observed and strictly regulated test of relevant virtues. The condemned gladiator received the wooden sword of freedom from the emperor as the community shouted its approval stands as an enduring symbol of sport's ancestral ties to philosophy.

Those who seek to critically examine and improve sport today should remember to recognize the ancient Olympic resemblance between sport and philosophical inquiry. This connection recalls the important social and educational functions of ancient Greek athletics, and it challenges us to preserve the integrity of sport as a knowledge-seeking practice capable of serving noble human ends. We should appreciate sport's capacity for social subversion and its potential for individual education. This requires the humility to ask authentic questions and the courage to let the contest answer them impartially. Finally, we need to preserve public confidence in results by enforcing the rules of the contest no less rigorously than in scientific study. We should view sport as a knowledge-seeking activity capable of serving social and educational goals, as it did in Ancient Olympia.

Marble statue of Heracles, 69–96 CE.
Metropolitan Museum of Art number 03.12.13. Open access image.

Athletes:

Ancient Olympia's Athletic Heroes

To understand the ancient Olympic conception of an athlete, you might begin by writing down the name of a modern Olympic hero, then list the reasons for your choice. Most people's reasons involve athletic performance: gold medals, world records, improbable comebacks. Some focus on moral character: overcoming adversity and helping others on the field and off it. Other reasons might be related to group identities: nations, ethnicities, those with disabilities, and so on. Think about how this hero has benefitted you personally and others you care about. Then reflect on how you learned their story, and how you have shared it with others.

Now let me pour cold water over those warm and fuzzy thoughts by asking whether any athlete *really* deserves to be called a hero at all. In a world where first responders routinely risk their lives to search for earthquake survivors, rescue flood victims, or help the ailing to battle deadly diseases, it hardly seems heroic to hurdle a high bar. Olympic athletes do not heal the sick, rescue the stranded, or save lives. If your hero does, then their heroism hardly seems to be specifically "Olympic." What (if any) is the benefit provided by modern Olympic heroes, and how should we choose and think about the people that we count as such?

To answer that question, we might begin by examining the link between heroes and athletics in Ancient Greece. This is useful not just because our modern Games have their roots in Ancient Olympia, but also because heroes like Heracles had an important educational function there—one linked with athletics and justly criticized by Socrates and others. Ancient Greek heroes were human, not just in the sense that they were mortal but also in the sense of being flawed. Nevertheless, their stories served as inspiring ethical paradigms. Heracles' labors are even chiseled into the metopes of Olympia's grand Temple of Zeus and can be seen in its museum today.

Let us begin by examining the heroic spirit in ancient Greece, see how it was linked to sport and the celebration of victory, and consider the risks and rewards of this system as moral education. Then we can return to the question of modern Olympic heroes, examining if and how they too may function as moral educators in light of this ancient heritage and modern Olympic realities. In the process, we will discover the value of an "athletic ethos" that demands voluntary struggle on behalf of the greater good, which is motivated and compensated by the public celebration of *aretē* (excellence, virtue).

Hero Worship as Moral Education

The first point of resemblance between ancient Greek heroes and modern Olympic athletes is that their achievements inspire others to strive for excellence in their own lives. In the ethical systems based on virtue prevalent in ancient Greece, people who provide paradigms of *aretē* (virtue, excellence) function as moral educators. The struggles and ordeals that demonstrated ancient heroes' *aretē* were called *athla*, but originally they had nothing to do with sport. In English, we call Heracles' *athla* "labors," a translation that rightly emphasizes their difficulty and benefit to the community. In Greek, they were also called *ponoi,* a term that evokes the idea of effort and exertion, and *agōnes,* the word used even today for athletic contests—including the *Olympiakoi Agōnes* (Olympic Games).

Even though the ancient poet Pindar credits Heracles with founding the Olympic Games, and the historian Diodorus says he won every inaugural event, the hero's *athla* were not sporting. Rather it was by slaying the Nemean lion, cleaning the stables of Augeas, and subduing various other animals and monsters that Heracles demonstrated his heroic *aretē.*

Ancient Greek heroes were mortals who performed *athla* so amazing that they suggested divine ancestry—in this sense they are prototypical *athl*etes. Athletes who competed in the ancient Olympic Games, however, were *not* considered heroes (at least, not at first). Rather, they were emulating the *athla* of heroes like Heracles as a form of moral education—in order to cultivate and demonstrate their own *aretē*.

Heroes and their mythological *athla* not only predate athletic festivals like the Olympic Games, sport itself may have emerged from hero cults. These were usually local, and worship took place near the tomb containing the hero's corpse, which was thought to have life-giving, talismanic powers. In order to activate those powers, worshippers performed rituals including *mimēsis* (re-enactment, emulation) of the hero's *athla* and placing *stephanoi* (wreaths of vegetation) on the tomb. Originally, these rituals were probably not sport and the wreaths were not victory crowns. However, Homer's *Iliad*, our earliest literary account of sport, depicts the rituals honoring the fallen hero Patroclus as athletic contests.

The conceptual link between sport and heroes helps us to understand the philosophy of ancient Greek athletics, especially its function as moral education. Rituals honoring heroes differ from those for gods and ancestors in that heroes are *chosen* for worship on the basis of their achievements. If moral education, at its most basic level, is simply the communication of collective ideas about how we ought to live and the kind of people we ought to be, then a community's decision to worship a hero fits that description.

The transition from localized hero worship to nationwide festivals like the Olympic Games was likely part of a Panhellenizing tendency in the Archaic Period (roughly the 8th to early 5th centuries BCE)—one which transformed local rituals and ethical ideas into a national culture. Increased contact among formerly isolated communities led first to the exchange of beliefs, then the negotiation of more common beliefs. The localized songs of different Hellenic communities were consolidated into the Homeric and Hesiodic songs, and since these told the stories not only of gods but also and especially of heroes, a more universalized idea of how we should live and what kind of people we should be took shape.

Another way to say this is to claim that a distinctively Hellenic identity took shape, one that embraced an athletic ethos derived not from sport but from the *athla* of "national heroes" celebrated in mythology, universalizing poems, and eventually Panhellenic religious festivals like the Olympic Games. I have characterized this convergence of sport, art, and religion as a cultural conspiracy to promote *aretē*. What is important to notice here is that ancient Greek athletics derives from rituals celebrating the *athla* of fallen heroes and these celebrations functioned as moral education by communicating an ideal of *aretē* that was characterized by an athletic ethos.

Heracles and the Athletic Ethos

The athletic ethos that links sport and moral education in ancient Greece can be summarized succinctly as "voluntary struggle for the sake of excellence," and can be illustrated by Heracles, a hero celebrated by athletes even today. In ancient culture, he also inspires philosophers and politicians—as well as popular morality. The story of Heracles, like all Greek heroes, involves progression from imperfection toward perfection, from humanity toward divinity, or, in Platonic terms, from the real toward the ideal.

The metaphysical background for this is eloquently expressed in Hesiod's *Works and Days* (109-175) where gold, silver, and bronze generations of humanity are followed by a generation of semi-divine heroes who are better and more just than other human beings. Heroes do not begin in the perfected state of the golden generation (much less as gods). Rather, they recognize their imperfection and attempt, though *aretē*, to better resemble their glorious ancestors.

Terracotta neck-amphora of Heracles wrestling the Nemean Lion as Athena looks on. Attributed to the Diosphos Painter ca. 500 BCE. Metropolitan Museum of Art number X.21.15. Open access image.

Though the Disney version of Heracles' story makes him the legitimate son of Zeus and Hera, in the ancient version his mother is the mortal Alcmene and Hera is the jilted wife who thwarts her husband's plan to make his son king. She gets Zeus to swear that any son of his born the day that Heracles was due shall reign over men, then she delays Heracles' birth and speeds up that of his cousin Eurystheus, who becomes king instead and proceeds to saddle Heracles with all kinds of unpleasant tasks. The hero is challenged not only by the injustice of his situation, but also by his personal shortcomings. He never seems to lack strength but is occasionally bereft of intelligence (*mētis*) and judgment (*krisis*). At one point, in a fit of madness induced by Hera, he goes so far as to slay his own wife and children

Such heroic excess is neither excused nor endorsed by Greek mythology. The point is that heroes are imperfect— human, if you will—and whatever divine gifts they may have, they face challenges involving antagonists (i.e., opponents in the *agōn*): human, divine, or even the allegorical personifications of intangible opponents like old-age and death. It is through voluntary engagement in such struggles— by performing *athla*—that the hero progresses toward the ideal. These *athla* demand *ponos* (effort, toil), which is voluntarily undertaken in the understanding that short-term suffering is needed to relieve greater suffering.

An *athlos* such as killing the Nemean lion, furthermore, not only solves a community problem, it also improves the hero's capacity to solve even more difficult problems—that is, their personal *aretē*. The athletic ethos is not simply about achieving a particular result, but also about improving as an individual through the process of taking on increasingly difficult and meaningful challenges. It is no accident that Heracles' *athla* become increasingly complex: in the first he must kill a single lion, in the last he faces a whole series of trials on his way to the underworld to capture its fearsome guard-dog Cerberus.

It is also important to note that these *athla* challenge the hero in a variety of ways. The problem cannot be solved merely with strength (*bia*), intelligence (*mētis*), or even clear vision (*theoria*); rather all the hero's virtues need to be coordinated harmoniously in order to complete the task. This is why *aretē* is best translated as "excellence," it engages and applies to multiple human capacities.

We can also talk about particular *aretai* (excellences) such as courage; in a way heroes are braver than immortals because they have to risk death to accomplish great things. Achilles concludes that he must actually *die* in order to achieve the *kleos* (glory) he desires. But it takes more than just courage to accomplish the kind of feats that are immortalized in poetry. And even for those born with divine blood, such *aretē* must be achieved—or at least demonstrated—through performance.

Heracles' *athla* result in *apotheosis*—actually becoming a god—whereas Achilles and others become immortal in the sense that their story is told and retold in songs like Homer's *Iliad*. Such celebrations of heroic *aretē* function as an *athlon* (prize) that both motivates and rewards the performance of *athla*. And, as is characteristic of the athletic ethos, this kind of prize benefits not just the hero but also the community. The stories, songs, and statues dedicated to heroes (not to mention athletes) inspire others to strive for excellence themselves. This provides a greater benefit to people over time than any single accomplishment ever could.

To summarize the athletic ethos that links heroes, athletes, and moral education, then: the original *athlete* is someone who voluntarily engages in painful struggles to improve themselves and their community; the performance of these *athla* cultivates and demonstrates an exemplary level of *aretē*, which is then rewarded and celebrated publicly with an *athlon* in the form of a prize, statue, or song. Not only does the practice of athletics in ancient Greece borrow its structure and vocabulary from this heroic ethos, it adopts and enhances its educational function.

Atalanta and Athletic *Mimēsis*

Historically speaking, the story told by Diodorus Siculus in the 2nd century CE of Heracles inaugurating the Olympic Games by competing in and winning every event is nonsensical. By 776 BCE, the traditional founding date of the Games, the hero had long since gone to live with the gods on Olympus. Conceptually speaking, however, Diodorus' story makes perfect sense: Heracles sets the example for Olympic athletes to follow. It doesn't matter what the particular contests are or when they were added to the program because Olympic athletes are not emulating Heracles as an athlete in the sporting sense, but rather in the heroic sense just discussed.

That is to say, athletes emulate Heracles' "athletic ethos" in the effort to approximate (if not achieve) his *aretē*. Thus, heroic *athla* inspire athletic *agōnes* with one key distinction. Heroes' *athla* become public through the telling of their stories, but athletic *agōnes* are performed publicly for educational benefit through a process of *mimēsis* and *katharsis* (cleansing, clarification). By imitating (and celebrating) the *athla* of fallen heroes, athletes and spectators at the Olympic Games clarified their understanding of heroic *aretē*.

Let me illustrate this transition from *athla* to *agōnes* with the example of Atalanta, the ancient Greek heroine famous for losing a race for her hand in marriage. This example may seem un-Olympic since women did not compete in the ancient Olympic Games, but there were races for *parthenoi* (unmarried women) on the Olympic track and, by Hellenistic times, in all of the other Panhellenic festivals. I think it is plausible that those running *parthenoi* were emulating Atalanta.

The gist of Atalanta's story is that she was abandoned as a baby because her father wanted a boy, then raised by a bear and hunters in the woods. She grew up to be one of the *aristoi* (best) of the Hellenes and participated with valor in such ventures as the Calydonian boar hunt. Some of her *athla* even resemble those of Heracles. For example, her clever slaying of Hylaeus and Rhoecus, centaurs who came to rape her, reflects Heracles' famed confrontations with centaurs—one of whom is identified as Hylaeus in a 6th century BCE vase painting.

Devoted to the divine *parthenos* Artemis, Atalanta resisted marriage. But despite, or perhaps because of this, she attracted many suitors. Either she or her father came up with a scheme to give her hand to any man who could beat her in a footrace. But she was very fast and defeated them all, until a hero named Hippomenes used a combination of *mētis* (cunning) and divine assistance to defeat her. As she pulled ahead in the race, he rolled golden apples given to him by Aphrodite (a symbol courtship and marriage) in front of Atalanta, who slowed to pick them up and was ultimately defeated. The story may seem to prove Hippomenes' *aretē* more than Atalanta's—and this is part of the point. Atalanta's resistance to her suitors reflects the "athletic ethos" of engaging in struggle for the sake of excellence and—in her case—winning the *athlon* of a heroic husband and ultimately a heroic son.

Footraces for *parthenoi* in ancient Greece may have been designed to emulate Atalanta's athleticism and educationally evoke her virtues. Like other contests, these races began as religious rituals designed to mark the transition from girlhood to maidenhood, i.e., eligibility for marriage. Through *mimēsis* of Atalanta's marriage race, girls could experience some approximation of the heroine's *athlos* and thereby improve their understanding of her virtue—a result known as *katharsis*, understood (as in the case discussed above) as the clarification of ideas and not just ritual purification.

White-Ground Lekythos with Atalanta running from Eros.
Attributed to Douris (500–490 BCE)
The Cleveland Museum of Art, open access image.

It takes courage, self-control, and other forms of *aretē* to run a race well and, more importantly, to navigate the challenges of adolescence and courtship. This is true for males and females alike, and it explains not only the educational function of athletics, but also their religious purpose in places like Ancient Olympia.

Sometimes the myths reenacted by sport are obvious, for example the *apobatēs* race at the Panathenaic Games recreates an event from the war with the Titans in which the goddess Athena attacks from a rushing chariot. Often the resemblance is not so clear: are wrestlers imitating Heracles with the lion? Are discus throwers channeling Odysseus? Do javelin throwers imagine themselves fighting in the Trojan War? It doesn't matter. The real thing being emulated is the *aretē* of the heroes, or more specifically their "athletic ethos." Athletic games are just constructs designed to provide a challenge sufficient to evoke *aretē*—or at least some facsimile of it.

The Power of the Prize: *Athlon* and *Kudos*

The *athlon*, which serves as motivation and reward for the heroic *athlos*, is also replicated in sport. In the *Iliad*, Achilles sets out prizes to initiate each athletic contest. But we should not limit our conception of an *athlon* to the material token offered to victors—these are merely symbolic of an immaterial thing that is more valued. At its most general level, the *athlon* is the improved state of affairs brought about by the hero's *athlos*. The benefit of Heracles' *athla* goes primarily to the community, though the hero ultimately received the personal *athlon* of *apotheosis*. Even heroes who were not divinized sometimes received cult after their death—rituals expected to benefit the community by celebrating heroic *aretē*.

This cycle of achievement, benefit, and celebration that motivates further achievement is central to the "athletic ethos." In ancient sport, it was replicated through what Leslie Kurke calls the "economy of *kudos*." Just as an epic hero's *athla* were motivated and then compensated by the glory received through his song, the Olympic athlete is motivated and compensated by the public celebration of his victory. This ceremony transferred the victor's *kudos*—a talismanic power that brought good fortune in battle—to his city. The olive crown given to victors at the Olympic Games was symbolic of this beneficial power, which held more value for the athlete and his city than any material prize ever could.

The civic value of the victor's *kudos* explains why ancient athletes' victory celebrations involved fancy parades, erecting monuments, even partially dismantling city walls. They also included the performance of *epinician* (victory) songs that lauded the athlete's *aretē*—not least by connecting him with mythological heroes. It was common to shower victors with honors and gifts including front-row seats at civic events and *sitēsis*—meals for life at government expense.

In some cases, the mysterious powers of victorious athletes were attributed to their statues: that of the pankratist Polydamas, for example, was said to be capable of healing the sick. Meanwhile, the boxer Theagenes' statue was disrespected to the point of being whipped, then tried for murder after it fell on its assailant and killed him. The statue was convicted and thrown into the sea, but later the city was forced to retrieve it and worship the athlete as a hero in order to end a famine. In fact, several athletes were worshipped as heroes after their deaths—a phenomenon that reinforces this conceptual link. The motivation for their worship was not athletic performance, but concern about community welfare.

We need not resort to legends about healing statues or talismanic powers to explain how communities benefit from recognizing and celebrating the *aretē* of athletes (and heroes), however. We already observed that Greek athletics reenacted heroic *athla* by constructing contests that demanded authentic *aretē*, a process of *mimēsis* that led to the *katharsis* of clarified understanding of human excellence. Plato might even describe the process as *anamnēsis*, the recollection of innate knowledge sparked by a worldy experience. In this case, the experience of athletic struggle would cause us to recollect our innate understanding of ideal *aretē*.

The public celebration of athletic victors functioned analogously. By identifying as a group with the victorious athlete's *aretē,* the community was able to motivate the cultivation of *aretē* among its young—especially the choruses of young men and women who moved rhythmically as a group while they sang the athlete's praises. The link between athlete and hero is revived by the song, and the sacred moment of victory when *kudos* was conferred is made eternal by a statue or inscribed memorial. Such inscriptions often repeated the words announced in the victory ceremony, thereby re-enacting the moment of glory—and the athlete's heroic spirit—when read aloud. Like the worship of heroes, the celebration of victorious athletes functioned as moral education by inspiring the cultivation of *aretē.*

Socrates and Criticism of the System

Predictably, there were serious doubts in ancient Greece about the value of athletic victory—especially the richness of its rewards. Among the first critics was the philosopher Xenophanes, who said in Fragment 2, "It is not right to prefer strength to my good wisdom" because Olympic victory does not bring better laws or "fatten the storerooms" of the city:

> If a man wins a victory with swiftness of foot or in pentathlon where the precinct of Zeus lies beside the streams of Pisa in Olympia, or in wrestling or engaging even in painful boxing, or in the dread contest that they call pankration, and would be glorious for his townsmen to look upon and would win prominent pride of place in the contests, and would receive bread from the public larder of the city and a gift that would be a treasure for him, if even with horses he would obtain all these things, he would not be as worthy as I. Better than strength of men and horses is my wisdom. Those opinions are ill-

considered. It is not right to prefer strength to my good wisdom. Even if a man good at boxing be among the people, even if a man good at pentathlon or wrestling, even if in swiftness of foot, which is held in pride of place in whatever deeds of men's strength belong to the contest, not for that reason would the city have better laws. Small joy would it be for the city if an athlete wins beside the banks of Pisa, for this does not fatten the storerooms of the city.

It is plausible to interpret Xenophanes' skepticism about the value of athletic victory as part of his general criticism of religious beliefs—especially if mysterious powers like *kudos* were involved.

The identification of athletics with religious worship in ancient Greece also influenced city politics, and it was in this context that the more famous philosopher Socrates reprised Xenophanes' criticism of civic rewards for athletes. Having been convicted in Athens of impiety (the requested penalty for which was death), Socrates responds in Plato's *Apology* that what he really deserved for his service to the city was *sitēsis*, the public sustenance awarded to Olympic victors. The philosopher's rationale was that the victors only made the citizens "seem" happy, whereas he made them happy in reality. The term Socrates uses, *eudaimōn*, indicates a happiness characterized not just by pleasure but also divine blessing—the kind of thing sought through athletic ritual.

Since Socrates is among the founders of ancient Greek virtue ethics, his rejection of the idea that Olympic victors benefit communities seems to challenge the argument that athletics functioned as moral education based on the *mimēsis* and *katharsis* of *aretē*. However Socrates contrasts the value of his public questioning about the nature of *aretē* with the benefit provided by victors in Olympic chariot races—which is to say wealthy horse-owners who did not actually compete but received the victory crown and all its attendant privileges.

So part of Socrates' complaint seems to be that people who haven't demonstrated *aretē* unfairly receive the celebration due to those who have—a practice clearly contrary to the athletic ethos. Epinician poets like Pindar routinely attributed heroic *aretē* to equestrian victors, who paid them handsomely to do so not least because it served their political interests. The Sicilian tyrants, in particular, commemorated their chariot victories sumptuously with songs, statues, and celebrations that reinforced their political power. Perhaps Socrates had this hypocrisy in mind when he denigrated the civic value of Olympic victors in comparison with his educational labors.

Of course, Socrates did not compete in the Games either, but he exemplified the athletic ethos of engaging in a struggle for the sake of *aretē*; he even died for it and was immortalized heroically in Plato's dialogues. A clarified understanding (*katharsis*) of *aretē* was Socrates' goal as a moral educator and he performed his service in gymnasia, even if Socratic *agōn* took the form of questioning rather than athletic *mimēsis*.

Plato famously criticized *mimēsis* as thrice removed from truth, though he agrees with Aristotle that it is though experience of likenesses that we come to understand the truths they represent. Would Plato accept the *mimēsis/katharsis* model of moral education through athletics?

Apparently so. His rationale for excluding poets in the *Republic* is that their stories of gods and heroes include vicious behavior that children shouldn't be exposed to—the myth of Pelops, who cheated in chariot race to win dominion over Olympia, is even cited as an example. But both the *Republic* and *Laws* give prominent place to gymnastics and athletics as means of cultivating *aretē*. As a result, I think Plato would endorse the athletic *mimēsis* of heroic *athla* as long as only virtuous actions are emulated.

31

Likewise, Plato would consider Socratic questioning to be an athletic activity that provides educational challenges. The *experience* of competing against stronger opponents clarifies our understanding of heroic *aretē* precisely by demanding a lesser version of it. It also integrates youth into the cultural paradigm of pursuing *aretē* by adopting an athletic ethos.

Modern Olympic Heroes

So in addition to the model for modern sport, Ancient Olympia offers us an athletic ethos that provides a robust educational link between heroes and athletes based on *aretē*. It was a system in which heroes exemplified *aretē,* athletes strove to cultivate it, and communities were improved by celebrating it. Might a similar formula justify the idea of modern Olympic heroes? There are major differences to be accounted for. The modern Olympic Movement is international and multicultural, so the *aretē* of its heroes has to be universal. Also, if athletes themselves function as heroes in this modern system, then who does the emulating, and what benefit do they provide?

We are *not* talking here about athletes being role models, since the role of elite athlete can be played by precious few and is not intrinsically valuable to society. Rather, we should view Olympic heroes as "character models" who are selected and celebrated in a way that benefits society.

As in ancient Greece, it is the athletic ethos of Olympic heroes and not their athletic achievements that should be celebrated and emulated. The role of sport is to set up challenges that provide non-heroes the opportunity to cultivate through experience the kinds of courage, self-control, respect, and persistence required to be effective in responding to meaningful challenges outside of sport.

Conclusion

The modern Olympic festival, like globalized sport in general, has become so large and successful that it can seem like a world unto itself, detached from social and ethical concerns. As in ancient Olympia, however, the celebration of heroes by any group functions as moral education—even when that group is the global community.

The question we have considered is whether Olympic athletes deserve to be celebrated as heroes in a world where first responders routinely risk their lives for the benefit of others. By analyzing the link between heroes and athletes in ancient Greece, we identified an "athletic ethos" that promoted voluntary struggle for the sake of excellence—both of the individual and his or her community.

We observed that athletes emulated heroes by engaging in struggles of increasing difficulty and importance, and that communities inspired others to cultivate excellence by celebrating athletic victories. We learned that the system was criticized by philosophers, but only when it posited mysterious powers or confused authentic *aretē* with mere athletic success. And finally, we observed that modern Olympic athletes may function analogously to ancient Greek heroes by inspiring us to adopting that ancient "athletic ethos" with a view to making ourselves and our world the best it can be.

Fragments of a marble statue of the Diadoumenos,
Roman copy of a Greek original attributed to Polykleitos.
Metropolitan Museum of Art #25.78.56. Open access image.

Excellence:

Nudity as the Costume of *Aretē* in Ancient Olympia

Is it possible, despite dramatic changes in the *practice* of Olympic sport over the last three millennia, that the ethical values underpinning it have endured? One way to explore that question is by examining what appears to be the starkest difference between the ancient and modern Olympic Games: athletic nudity. Does the naked Olympic athlete represent a primitive original state from which modern athletes have evolved? Does athletic nudity symbolize an ethos of purity and naturalism inevitably lost in this era of professionalism and performance-enhancement? Or does it represent a persistent and enduring ethos that can be detected in the ideals of Modern Olympism and serve as a meaningful criterion for the management of modern sport?

Interestingly enough, the earliest athletes did not compete nude, and explanations for the introduction of athletic nudity at the ancient Olympic Games include apparently "modern" concerns about performance enhancement and safety. The 2nd century CE travel writer Pausanias tells us that Orsippus of Megara initiated the practice by winning the footrace after losing his loincloth. "My own opinion," Pausanias adds, "is that at Olympia he intentionally let the girdle slip off him, realizing that a naked man can run more easily than one girt" (1.44.1). On the face of it, this story seems plausible since we commonly think of athletes as willing to do anything and everything to improve their performance.

The historian Dionysius of Halicarnassus (7.72) concurs that the runner intentionally dropped his shorts, adding that before the incident Greeks were ashamed to appear naked at the Games. Apparently, Olympic victory was sufficient to remove such shame—an epitaph for Orsippus suggests that he even went nude to the victory ceremony. By Isidorus' account

(18.17.2), safety was the motivation for athletes competing nude: the magistrate Hippomenes decreed they do so after a runner tripped over his shorts. May we conclude from this Roman-era testimony that athletic nudity is just the first in a long line of attempts by athletes to enhance performance at the Olympic Games? Or was it an attempt to ensure safety? It turns out that nudity's explanation has more to do with the link between sport and virtue.

Athletic nudity in the ancient Olympic Games expressed an ethos of human excellence that actively eschews performance-enhancing technologies (and isn't too worried about safety). In fact, athletic performance was neither measured quantitatively nor valued intrinsically in ancient times; its value derived from what the Greeks called *aretē* (excellence, virtue). The ancient Olympic ethos of *aretē* was characterized by respect for ideals, public demonstration, individual effort, and civic responsibility—values that persist today. The naked Olympic athlete of ancient Greece is more than a relic of the past on this view, he is a symbol of unassisted human potential voluntarily engaged in a struggle for excellence that benefits both individual and community.

Nudity as the Costume of Gods and Heroes

Nudity at the Olympic Games was neither primitive nor original; by all accounts it was deliberately introduced around the 15th Olympiad or 720 BCE, more than 50 years after the traditional founding of the Games. Before that, athletes presumably competed in loincloths (*zomata*) that covered their genitals, as they had in Homer's epics—our earliest written account of Greek athletics. Outside of sport and certain religious rituals, nudity was and always had been considered shameful in Greek society. When Homer's Odysseus washes up nude on the island of the Phaeacians, he rushes to cover himself lest he be viewed naked by the locals. The goddesses Athena and Artemis cursed mortals who saw them nude with blindness or death. Even male deities and heroes usually appear clothed in Hellenic art before the 7th century BCE.

So athletic nudity was clearly an intentional choice that had enough symbolic meaning to override the original and predominant impulse to cover oneself in public. It was, in effect, a costume: something worn to create a particular appearance. In short, ancient athletes made a statement with their nudity: one that varied over time but was consistently connected with *aretē*.

To be sure, in athletics, *aretē* is linked with performance and Olympic victory was taken to be an affirmation of one's *aretē*. Nevertheless, Pausanias' explanation of nudity in terms of performance enhancement fails upon closer inspection. To begin, it is hard to see how sprinting naked could constitute an advantage over running in a loincloth—especially one that falls off at the beginning of a 200-meter race. It is even harder to see how uncovered genitals could provide a performance advantage in wrestling, boxing, or pankration.

Improved performance also fails to account for trainers' nudity—a phenomenon Pausanias explains with a fanciful yarn about the widow Kallipatera defying the ban on women at the Games by disguising herself as a trainer to watch her son compete. When she leapt out of the trainers' enclosure after her son's victory, her garment got caught in the fence and her gender was revealed. After that, says Pausanias, they passed a law that trainers should be naked—apparently to avoid future female infiltrators (5.6.7-8).

The story could be true, but it makes little sense as a rationale for trainers' nudity. If the goal was to protect the Olympic sanctuary from female infiltrators, shouldn't spectators be naked, too? And since when is removing a loincloth necessary to determine gender? Even though we may never know its true origin, the custom of nudity at Olympia probably had more to do with religion than performance.

We must always bear in mind that the ancient Olympic Games were primarily a religious festival, and athletic contests originated as a ritual *mimēsis* (imitation, emulation) of heroic *athla* (labors, feats, ordeals). The ritual functioned much like an invocation does in church today; indeed, a really outstanding athletic performance may well have been experienced by worshippers at the Olympic Games as an *epiphany*, the mystical appearance of the god or hero himself. The religious goal of athletics, then, was to invoke heroic *aretē* in order to benefit the community, as the mythological *athla* of heroes had. To be sure, athletics was at least one order removed from the *athla* of heroes like Heracles, but it signaled the presence of divine *aretē* in nature—and perhaps in the athlete himself.

It seems plausible, in light of such ritual, that athletic nudity was introduced into the Olympic Games in religious imitation of gods and heroes. The connection is powerfully illustrated in Greek art by the many "god or athlete" statues, which appear around the same time as athletic nudity. The very first of these were *kouroi*, 7th century BCE images ranging from small bronze figurines to larger-than-life statues (their female counterparts, like female athletes, wear clothing). Based on their headbands, some scholars believe they represent athletes (a *tainia* was tied around the victor's head at the conclusion of contests and served to distinguish athletes in classical art). Others claim that *kouroi* are statues of the god Apollo. Both interpretations support the idea that the costume of nudity connects athletes with gods and heroes.

The runner-god Hermes is conventionally represented nude alongside Heracles at the Greek gymnasium. Naked athletes appear in vase painting as early as the 7th century BCE and become common by the mid-6th century BCE. Nudity remained shameful in Greek culture outside of sport, however. It must have been the divinely sanctioned *aretē* of gods and heroes that made nudity an acceptable and even desirable costume for athletes. In the words of Plato (*Republic* 457a), they "wear virtue instead of clothes."

So Orsippus would have felt no shame being crowned naked in Olympia because his victory had demonstrated the *aretē* that set him above the level of common humans and closer to heroes and gods. If, however, he had prevailed because of a performance-enhancing trick, then he would have been doubly ashamed; indeed he might have violated the athletes' sacred Olympic oath. The religious value of his athletic performance, like the value of Olympic victory itself, depended on it being derived from the *aretē* that the ritual was designed to evoke.

Athletic excellence was sometimes even taken to be a sign of divine heritage. Heracles revealed that he was the son of Zeus by strangling two serpents and saving his half-brother in their crib. As something divine, furthermore, the *aretē* that produced athletic excellence was inseparable in the Olympic context from moral excellence, and the beautiful athletic body was emblematic of goodness.

So athletic nudity, first of all, is the costume of *aretē,* which connects human beings with the gods and heroes. Olympic victory celebrates this *aretē* (not least by crowning the athlete with leaves sacred to Zeus), but only after that *aretē* has been demonstrated athletically.

Nudity as the Costume of (Demonstrated) Aristocracy

We don't know whether ancient Olympic victors mounted a podium as they do today, but the sense that victory elevates an individual above their peers is part and parcel of the Olympic ethos. So is the sense that all eyes are on the victor—even divine eyes. The ontology of *aretē* is hierarchical, with the gods occupying the top of the scale, heroes appearing just below them, and human beings below that. Athletes could be imagined as struggling to climb from the human level upward toward the divine.

Olympic victory, furthermore, was regarded as a gift from the gods. The winner's crown was delivered from above by the goddess Nike—as depicted by the famous statue in Ancient Olympia's museum—and the victorious athlete was expected to dedicate part of his reward to the gods in thanksgiving. In short, Olympic victory represented divine recognition of demonstrated *aretē*.

Ariston, an Olympic victor in the pankration is portrayed in his monument as standing before the house of Zeus to be greeted by him and the river-god Alpheios (Olympia lies at the intersection of the Alpheios and Kladeos rivers). The inscription makes it clear that the victory itself was earned through demonstration of his excellence:

> Greece said [I] was perfect when she saw me, though still a boy, with the *aretē* of men, victorious with my blows. A winner not by the luck of the draw, but without a bye. (*Epigr. auf Sieger*, 79)

Implicit in the idea of excellence is the drive, as Homer sings, "to be the best and outdo all others" (*Iliad* 6.208, 11.784). The word in Greek for "best" is *aristos* and in this way Olympic victory was associated with aristocracy. Athletes' social ranking was visible in public processions, where those who won important contests held prestigious positions just behind the high priests and top officials. Unlike other forms of social ranking, however, this place in the procession was earned. Even when aristocratic *aretē* was considered hereditary, it demanded public demonstration.

Odysseus himself, among the foremost Hellenic heroes, repeatedly uses athletic performance to demonstrate his *aretē*, thereby affirming his nobility. In the funeral games of the *Iliad*, he enters the wrestling (which ends in a draw) then goes straight on to win the footrace (with Athena's help). In the *Odyssey*, he is reluctant to participate in the games of the

Phaeaecians, having spent his days at sea on a raft. But when the youthful Euryalos challenges his aristocratic identity by suggesting that he is a greedy merchant rather than an athlete, the hero grabs a discus and hurls it far beyond the others' marks. He then invites the locals to challenge him in any athletic contest, noting that their only chance at defeating him is in the footrace because his knees have been battered by his time at sea.

Odysseus, in fact, is the reigning monarch of Ithaca, but when he finally arrives home no-one recognizes him except his dog. It is by demonstrating his athletic skills in boxing and archery (not to mention stringing the royal bow) that he proves who he is and takes back his kingdom. The point here is that the connection among athletic performance, *aretē,* and aristocracy is not taken for granted, it demands demonstration before the eyes of one's peers as well as the gods. In the ethos of the Olympic Games, aristocracy merges with meritocracy.

An aristocrat who stood naked before his competitors to be crowned Olympic victor would feel affirmed, not ashamed. Prominent Greek families routinely claimed divine blood, so Olympic victory was a way to confirm their status and validate their privilege. Standing naked on the starting line was surely another matter, however, since it meant subjecting oneself to public (as well as divine) scrutiny and risking one's reputation.

The case of the aristocrat Alcibiades is illuminating: he avoided the risk of defeat by entering seven teams in the Olympic four-horse chariot race of 416 BCE and won first, second, and fourth place (Thucydides 6.16.2). Meanwhile, he disdained participation in the "naked" events because many athletes were of low birth. Likewise, Alexander the Great, when asked whether he would compete at Olympia in the footrace, responded that he would as long as his competitors were also kings (Plutarch 4.9-11). The social pressure on aristocrats to demonstrate their "inborn" *aretē* athletically is

41

proven by the number of aristocrats who actually took the risk of open competition—and won.

We should be no more surprised that ancient Olympic victors came from wealthy families, however, than we are that modern Olympic victors tend to come from wealthy countries. As it does today, wealth provided a competitive advantage, and those who had it tried to exploit it to their own advantage. Engaging in sport in any epoch requires leisure time and economic resources. It was also true, as it is today, that the prestige of Olympic victory was such that members of the lower classes sought and eventually achieved it. Such victories could be explained by some secret divine ancestor, or by talent and training. Since the latter explanation undermined the idea that *aretē* was inherited, aristocratic athletes didn't advertise their training.

Not unlike the turn-of-century "amateur" ethos depicted in the film, *Chariots of Fire,* the use of coaches and trainers was initially concealed. Even Pindar, the poet who wrote victory odes for wealthy patrons all over the Greek world, rarely credits training for a victory. His tenth *Olympian* ode to the young Hagesidamus, winner in the boys' boxing in the Olympics of 476 BCE, claims that only those born with *aretē* can be trained to achieve Olympic victory. For Pindar, athletic *aretē* derives from blood connections to gods and heroes. He acknowledges that heredity alone is not sufficient, but he insists that athletic victory depends on divine favor.

Of course Pindar is writing for aristocratic patrons and many of his odes are for equestrian events, which were officially won by the horse-owner rather than the rider or charioteer. Equestrian events were added to the Olympic Games about 100 years after their founding, perhaps in an attempt to preserve the competitive advantages of wealth, which were no-doubt being eroded by lower-class victors in the *gymnic* (naked) events.

Indeed, the competitive advantages of wealth may explain why expensive technologies and sports (including equestrian events) remain a part of the modern Olympics. Horse races in the ancient Games seemed to preserve the "athletic" link between aristocracy and *aretē* without requiring personal demonstration; but the issue was predictably controversial.

After the horses owned by the Spartan princess Cyniska were victorious at the Olympic Games, she had a victory statue erected there that boasted "I am the only woman in all Greece who won this crown." According to Plutarch (20.1), however, Cyniska's brother, Agesilaos, pushed her to enter the team precisely because "he wanted to show the Greeks that an equestrian victory was the result of wealth and expenditure, not in any way the result of *aretē*."

Although the sponsorship of racing teams was considered *euergetism* (expenditure of wealth for community benefit), equestrian victories were hardly evidence of personal *aretē* the way victories in running or wrestling were. It is hard to believe that anyone—Zeus least of all—was deceived into equating the two. It is likewise hard to imagine that any horse-owner, even the notoriously beautiful Alcibiades, presented himself in the nude to collect his victory crown. The Greeks appreciated the difference between victory achieved through wealth and *athla* achieved through personal effort. The expression traceable to Homer's *Odyssey* 8.145 had enduring resonance: "There is no greater glory for a man so long as he lives than that which he achieves by his own hands and his feet."

Nudity as the Costume of Training

Despite the addition of equestrian events and the poetic attempts to attribute those victories to *aretē*, the "naked" events consistently brought the most Olympic glory. The fame of the wrestler Milo was such that, according to Diodorus Siculus (12.9.5-6), when he led Croton's outnumbered army into battle "wearing his [six] Olympic crowns and equipped with the gear

43

of Heracles," the citizens credited their victory to him. Perhaps the opposing Sybarites were awed enough to think that Heracles himself had appeared on the battlefield before them.

Unlike Heracles, however, Milo's *aretē* was not considered a matter of divine heritage; it was clearly a matter of training. Indeed, athletes from his hometown in southern Italy won so many Olympic victories in the 6th century BCE, that a proverb claimed, "the last of the Crotoniates was the first among all the other Greeks" (Strabo 6.1.12). The secret of Croton's success may well have been the invention of serious athletic training. The philosopher Pythagoras emigrated there from Samos and founded a cult-like community that focused on subjecting bodily impulses to the rule of reason.

The Pythagorean "way of life" included daily exercise, dietary restrictions, and religious ritual. Croton was also known for its medical expertise. That they employed—and maybe invented—progressive resistance training is suggested by the story that Milo, who was Pythagoras's son-in-law, lifted a calf every day until it was full-grown. As the classical period dawned, so did the idea that *aretē* was less an entitlement of birth than a product of training—of voluntary effort, or *ponos.*

Everyone knows that an athlete's naked beauty results not from a life of leisure, but rather from working out. Although gods were by definition perfect and had no need to train, the link between *aretē* and *ponos* wasn't new. Heracles' labors were called *ponoi,* and his apotheosis resulted from their performance, not luck or birthright. The growing popularity of athletics in the 6th and 5th centuries BCE, along with the link between victory are *aretē,* can only have underscored the idea that humans are made better by habitual individual *ponos.* This was exemplified in the training of future citizens in the *gymnasium.* The demonstration of *philoponia* (love of effort) was a key element of their training, and among the contests used to determine their progress.

The emphasis on *ponos* may also explain the requirement that Olympic hopefuls spend one month before the Games in full-time training at the nearby town of Elis. That much time away from work was difficult for poorer athletes, but sponsorship from cities and wealthy benefactors quickly emerged to take up the slack. The advantages of wealth were further undermined when Elis decided to compensate athletes during the training period. Hereditary aristocrats who had once tried to conceal their training, hired coaches and began frequenting public *gymnasia* alongside less-wealthy comrades who had earned citizenship through democratic reforms. In this new political environment, *aretē*—and the beautiful body that symbolized it—was not something inherited, but rather something to be earned personally with sweat.

The most serious form of cheating in the ancient Olympic Games was the attempt to replace *ponos* and *aretē* with money. In his description of Olympia, Pausanias describes a row of bronze statues of Zeus that flank the entrance to the stadium. These *zanes* were financed with the fines paid by cheating athletes. The problem was not, as translations often suggest, the simple breaking of rules, however.

Pausanias (5.21.2-13) says that the athletes "violated the contests"—using the verb connected to the religious vice of *hubris*—and in every case of cheating he discusses, money is the culprit. The first injustice (*adikēma*) done to the games was by Eupolus of Thessaly who bribed his competitors in boxing. In the second case, an Athenian pentathlete bought off his competitors and when the Athenians refused to pay the resulting fine and threatened to boycott the Games, none less than the god at Delphi intervened, refusing to deliver his oracles until the Athenians had paid.

Pausanias continues to detail cases of bribery among wrestlers and pankratiasts, finishing with the story of an Egyptian boxer who arrived at Elis too late for the training period described above. The athlete claimed to have been delayed by poor sailing weather, but a witness attested that he had been competing at money games in Ionia. The elegiac verses on these punishment statues state: "that an Olympic victory is to be won, not by money, but by swiftness of foot and strength of body" (5.21.4), and "the contest at Olympia is one of *aretē* and not of wealth" (5.21.7). There is even reason to believe that these verses were part of the oath taken by athletes (as well as judges and trainers) at the opening of the Olympic Games. Whether the athletes were nude when they took the oath, we do not know.

The practice of disrobing for athletic training (*gymnastikē*, literally: naked activity), symbolically strips the individual of his worldly attachments—including wealth. The *aretē* sought through training, like the beautiful body associated with it, is the product of personal agency, i.e., something autonomously chosen and brought about through our own efforts. In Aristotelian terms, *aretē* is a *hexis*—a dynamic state brought about by habitual *ponos* and realized through virtuous activity.

The methodical training familiar to athletes seems to have inspired the methodical pursuit of virtuous wisdom made famous by Socrates and Plato. Indeed Socratic method is often characterized by Plato as a *mimēsis* of athletic training, and *aretē* as the health (or perhaps fitness) of the soul, but since souls were thought to move bodies, gymnastic training was believed to beautify persons inside and out. The *aretē* connected with demonstrated aristocracy and Olympic victory was revealed by the Classical period to be a product of individual effort—something available, at least theoretically, to everyone.

The connection among virtue, training, and Olympic victory is illustrated in an inscription honoring Kallikrates, a pankratiast of the Imperial Period. We read in his monument that Kallikrates "followed the path of *aretē* from his earliest youth, [and] through sweat and effort (*ponos*) obtained great renown." The inscription says that he "came to be...admired by all men throughout the inhabited world for the complete wisdom which he obtained through his love of training." Kallikrates was also revered for his excellent physique and for "taking care of his soul" (*SEG* 48.906). The naked beauty of this athlete is more than skin-deep and the *aretē* it represents is clearly something earned—the product of personal agency, of the "way of life" for which he is congratulated.

Nudity characterized the beginning as well as the end of *aretē*. You had to strip to engage in *gymnastikē*, and it was through a way of life characterized by the voluntary effort known as *ponos* that you achieved the physique associated with *aretē*. The process, in short, was characterized by transparency: the virtue demonstrated by Olympic victory was expected to be the product of personal agency.

Nudity as the Costume of Civic Responsibility

The authenticity of the *aretē* recognized by Olympic victory—including the fairness and transparency of the process for achieving it—was also important because it was expected ultimately to serve the community. Like the heroes whose *athla* they emulate, athletes act individually on behalf of collective interests. As such, the *aretē* cultivated through sport was expected to apply beyond it. In this sense, the costume of athletic nudity was also a costume of civic responsibility.

Individuals who stripped themselves for training in the *gymnasium* were perceived to be dedicating their *ponos* to a greater good. Military service is an obvious example, but the social benefits of *aretē* go well beyond that, resembling what we now call leadership. This is why communities honored Olympic victors with monuments, statues, and even lifetime public subsistence—they wanted to promote the way of life that cultivated civic virtue. So *aretē* may be something cultivated individually, but it is celebrated collectively by the communities that benefit from it.

Panathenaic prize amphora depicting a horse race, ca. 490 BCE. Victory crowns in equestrian events were awarded to the owners rather than the rider or drivers of the horses. Metropolitan Museum of Art number: 56.171.3. Open Access image.

The honors that Greek cities paid to victorious athletes were sumptuous enough to attract the disapproval of such philosophers as Xenophanes and Socrates. Such criticisms were few, however, in comparison with the civic praise heaped on athletes like Damon of Andros, whose decree clearly formulates his victory in terms of community benefit. "The council and the people have decided," it begins, that because "Damon son of Philadelphos, a man virtuous and beautiful (*kalos kai agathos*)" favored the people (*dēmos*) with his victory, "the *dēmos* should crown him with a bronze image, due to his virtue (*aretē*)..." (*IG* 12 suppl. 257). Honorific inscriptions for athletes often share the same structure and language as those for other civic benefactors. This suggests not only that victory was seen more as a civic contribution than a personal achievement, but also that the *aretē* demonstrated in athletics was valued for its application beyond sport.

In fact, the Greek epigraphic record routinely touts *gymnasium* training as preparation to excel in civic leadership. The inscription for Polemaion of Kolophon, for example, begins by highlighting his time in the *gymnasium*, which "nourished his soul with the finest learning and trained his body in athletics." This training led to victories in the games, then to "taking charge of public affairs," seeking higher education in Rhodes, and finally serving as a city official in Smyrna, where he was praised for the "virtue (*aretē*) and orderliness of his life" (*SEG* 39.1243). In the post-classical *polis* especially, athletic rhetoric served as blueprint for civic benefactors to highlight their worthiness, whether they were athletes or not.

Collective interest in the cultivation of *aretē* that applies beyond sport is our best explanation for city sponsorship of *gymnasia* and support of successful athletes. The educational rivalry described in Aristophanes' 5th century BCE comedy *Clouds*—one that contrasts physically-fit self-controlled *gymnasium* youths with the flabby profligate tricksters of Socrates's "Thinkery"—was resolved in the 4th century BCE when Plato set up a school in the Academy gymnasium that combined intellectual and physical wrestling in the effort to produce *aretē*. In the *Republic* and *Laws*, Plato consistently justifies his gymnastic and athletic programs in terms of benefit to the state. "Athletes are what I want," says the Athenian lawgiver in *Laws* 830a, "competitors against a million rivals in the most vital struggles of all." The great struggles (*megistōn agōnōn*) he's talking about here are definitely *not* athletic *agōnes*.

The point is that athletic training and competition are beneficial insofar as they cultivate virtues transferable to more meaningful challenges in life. Not only is *ponos* fundamental for athletic training, it is crucial for success in civic endeavors. In Plato's *Republic*, performance in gymnastic contests is used to select candidates for higher education. "People's souls give up much more easily in hard study than in physical training," explains Socrates, reasoning that those who prove themselves willing to endure in the *gymnasium* will better serve the community (535b).

That citizens should be scrutinized naked in the *gymnasium* may seem harsh to modern sensibilities about privacy, but it has deep roots in Hellenic culture that are motivated by what we now call transparency. Aelian, a Roman author from the generation after Pausanias, reports in *Varia Historia* 14.7 that in Sparta future citizens presented themselves naked to the governing ephors, so that everyone could tell who was fit or flabby. Sparta, in fact, was (in)famous for public parades of naked youth. Most scandalous was the fact that females participated (Plutarch *Lycurgus* 14.3-4); the naked presentation of young men was widespread practice in the Hellenic world by the mid-6th century BCE.

Gymnasia even held contests that offered prizes for *euexia*, which some scholars call beauty contests because they were apparently based on appearance. The nudity in such contexts clearly had a symbolic value connected to *aretē*—the beautiful body was valued by the community because it represented virtues that were valued by the community.

Plato's *Gorgias* argues that souls being judged after death should be "stripped naked" of the clothing and worldly attachments which had hitherto deceived the judges, and that the judges too should be naked, "so that the judgement may be a just one" (523e). The text worries specifically about "wicked souls dressed in fine bodies." Nudity here, and in the culture of the *gymnasium*, implies transparency and authenticity.

As explained above, *aretē* is a hierarchical concept and nudity is a costume that reveals differences, but it was also associated with the democratizing tendency in Hellenic culture and in sport. Ancient Greek society was far from embodying the principles of equality embraced by the modern Olympic movement, but stripping people of their clothing stripped away the trappings of social hierarchy and functioned as a kind of symbolic equalizer. The *gymnasiarchic* law from Beroia, for example, specifically prohibited those lacking *aretē* to enter:

> The following shall not strip off [to exercise] in the *gymnasium*: a slave, a freedman and their sons, an *apalaistros* [physically unfit], a prostitute, anyone of those who have business at the marketplace, a drunk, and an insane person. (tr. Eran Lupu)

The fact that such a rule had to be set belies the fact that social outcasts may be indistinguishable from aristocrats once everyone is naked and working out.

Entrance to the *gymnasium* was in some sense a metaphor for civic participation. Indeed, inscriptions suggest that *gymnasium* officials occasionally allowed women and slaves to strip and train. Plato's *Republic* 457a argued that even women should exercise naked in the *gymnasium*, clothed by their *aretē*.

To some degree, athletic nudity laid the foundations upon which democracy was built in ancient Greece. In any case the city's legitimate interest in cultivating *aretē* applicable beyond sport were served by the authenticity and transparency implied by gymnastic nudity.

Conclusion

The value of Olympic victory—in ancient and modern times—depends not on athletic performance *per se,* but rather on the naked excellence that underpins it. The glory of athletes who won by bribery rather than *ponos,* as well as equestrian victors who demonstrated wealth rather than virtue, was diminished or stripped outright—and their examples were presented as warnings to others. Meanwhile, athletes who didn't win but still demonstrated *aretē* were praised. A pankratist named T. Claudios Rufos showed such virtue in the contest that he was allowed to set up a statue at Olympia (a privilege normally granted only to victors) and offered citizenship by the city of Elis (*Inschriften von Olympia* 54).

As organizers of the Olympic Games and hosts of the 30-day training period that preceded the festival, Elis knew as well as any community the value of *aretē.* Indeed it was from the ranks of their citizens that the Olympic officials, known as *Hellanodikai* (literally, judges of the Greeks), were chosen. Their task was ultimately a religious one, but it centered on ensuring that the contests honored the gods and heroes by reliably revealing and rewarding *aretē.* That *aretē* was the properly-demonstrated product of *ponos*—rather than an object of privilege or exchange—was a fundamental principle of the ancient Olympic Games.

The challenges faced by the Modern Olympic Movement are in some ways the result of the Games' extraordinary success. The benefits of Olympic victory have expanded well beyond statues, poetry, and civic honors. Indeed, the pursuit of Olympic medals by illegal means such as doping threatens to separate victory from the personal virtue that has always given it value. Meanwhile, the legal exploitation of superior wealth and technology to gain an advantage over less privileged competitors has the same effect. Any substance or technique that reduces an athlete's agency—the idea that he or she is the primary cause of his or her performance—undermines the enduring connection between victory and virtue upon which the Olympic ethos is based.

Because modern performance-enhancing technologies are often invisible, they thwart the demonstration requirement, permitting a public façade of moral responsibility while concealing an insider ethos of short-cuts and deception. The ancient Greeks acted as if everything was visible to the eagle-eyed god they honored at the Olympic Games. Athletes competed in the nude because they were expected to have nothing to hide, and the excellence symbolized by their naked bodies was itself divinely beautiful.

Statue of Atalanta running.
Copy of a Roman work by Pierre Lepautren, 1703–1705.
Photo: Jastrow (2007) Wikimedia Commons CC ID: 2631102

Women:

Women and Sport in Ancient Olympia

People who care about women in sport may be tempted to ignore its ancient Greek history and ideals. After all, the standard story about women and the ancient Olympic Games highlights their exclusion as athletes, coaches, officials, and even spectators. The ancient Greek model has even been used against women in the modern Movement, as suggested by a 1912 article called "Women at the Olympic Games" (included in the volume *Olympism*) in which Pierre de Coubertin states:

> the question of allowing women to participate in the Olympic Games has not been settled. The answer cannot be negative merely on the grounds that that was the answer in antiquity.

From this and similar comments, we might conclude that the best way to promote women in the Olympic Movement today is to distance ourselves from its ancient Greek heritage.

We would be making a big mistake. There is more to the story of women and sport in ancient Olympia, and it shows us, among other things, that the ancient Greek ideals that underpin the philosophy of the modern Olympic Games do not and never have applied only to men. Not only did females run footraces in Olympia from its earliest history, they also exemplified its philosophical ideals as heroes, administrators, and peacemakers. Those who care about women in the Olympic Movement today shouldn't reject its ancient Greek heritage, rather we should strive to appreciate women's involvement Olympic history and philosophy.

To do this we will need to engage both disciplines. By "ancient Olympic philosophy," I mean the ideals of humanism, justice, and peace that inspire the modern philosophy of Olympism outlined in the *Olympic Charter*, which guides the

Olympic Movement today. These *ideas* are evidenced in the art and literature that surrounds and underpins ancient Greek athletic culture. By "ancient Olympic history," I mean the *events* that took place, as evidenced by many of the same ancient literary sources, as well as related disciplines such as archaeology, epigraphy, and anthropology.

The key difference is that ideals are "normative" in that they indicate how people think things *ought to be*, while history is "descriptive," indicating how things actually were. Both disciplines are fallible, of course, and the distinction between them is somewhat artificial since ideas influence events, and events influence ideas.

But we cannot conclude from the historical fact that they did not compete alongside the men in the ancient Olympic Games, that women were also excluded from Olympic ideals. We need to ask history about the nature of and reasons for female exclusion, and we need to ask philosophy *how* to interpret its meaning. By critically questioning the ancient sources, we may better understand how women can thrive in the Olympic Movement today.

The Standard Story

There is evidence that females were present at the ancient Games, ran races on the Olympic track, and held politically important roles in local administration—yet the standard story in Olympic studies tends to focus on their exclusion. The (few) scholars who ask *why* women were excluded from competing alongside men generally attribute it to a misogynistic culture in which females were considered unathletic, undeserving of equal treatment, and incapable of political engagement.

Their evidence, almost always, comes from a single ancient source. More accurately, a single paragraph from the 2nd century CE travel writer Pausanias, which relates a colorful tale probably told to him by a tour-guide to pass the time on their journey toward Olympia:

As you go from Scillus along the road to Olympia, before you cross the Alpheius, there is a mountain with high, precipitous cliffs. It is called Mount Typaeum. It is a law of Elis to cast down it any women who are caught present at the Olympic games, or even on the other side of the Alpheius, on the days prohibited to women. However, they say that no woman has been caught, except Callipateira only; some, however, give the lady the name of Pherenice and not Callipateira. She, being a widow, disguised herself exactly like a gymnastic trainer, and brought her son to compete at Olympia. Peisirodus, for so her son was called, was victorious, and Callipateira, as she was jumping over the enclosure in which they keep the trainers shut up, bared her person. So her sex was discovered, but they let her go unpunished out of respect for her father, her brothers and her son, all of whom had been victorious at Olympia. But a law was passed that for the future trainers should strip before entering the arena. (5.6.7)

From this story, scholars plausibly conclude that women were prohibited from entering the Olympic sanctuary during the Games, that the exclusion was serious since death was the penalty for violating it, and that only one woman is known to have done so—though she was not killed in the end because she came from a family of Olympic champions.

Less plausibly, Callipateira's story is cited by the ancient writer Philostratus in *Gymnasticus* 17 to explain why trainers are nude at Olympia (and not elsewhere). Even less plausibly, Coubertin and others suggest that it explains why athletes competed in the nude, namely, for gender verification purposes, or, according to Coubertin's "Olympic Memoirs," (also cited in the *Olympism* volume), "in order more effectively to bar the weaker sex from the precincts of the competitions."

Using logic, one may extrapolate from the Callipateira story that no woman ever won an Olympic crown, and surmise that they did not compete in sports at all in ancient Greece. But these conclusions are false, and Pausanias himself dispels them both in the same text, where he discusses women who won Olympic crowns as horse-owners, and competed in footraces on the Olympic track for unmarried women (*parthenoi*) in a festival called the Heraea.

Pausanias also says *parthenoi* were allowed to watch the Games as spectators along with one married woman (*gynē*), the priestess of Demeter Chamyne, who had a special seat in the stadium. He even claims, in a persistently overlooked passage, that the "Sixteen Women" who organized the Heraea were politically responsible for creating and maintaining peace between Pisa and Elis, the two cities that administered the Olympic Games.

Some of the confusion about female exclusion is caused by translating the term *parthenoi* as "young girls" even though that status explicitly presents them as mature enough for marriage and motherhood. *Parthenoi* are not children and their presence at the Olympic Games, as well as in footraces at ancient Olympia and elsewhere, is not insignificant. Some scholars, believing that the presence of *parthenoi* seems to logically contradict the prohibition of women, attribute Pausanias' claim that *parthenoi* were allowed to watch the Games to the error of a scribe.

Instead, the seeming paradox caused by the claim that *parthenoi* participated as spectators should prompt us to philosophically interrogate the exclusion of women at the ancient Olympic Games. If such an exclusion was standard practice at all athletic festivals, then why did Pausanias (and his tour guide) feel the need to tell Callipateira's story? If athleticism was inappropriate or unbecoming for females in ancient Greek culture, why did *parthenoi* run races on the

Olympic track? If it was scandalous for unmarried women to see men naked, why were they allowed to watch any Games?

And what about married women (*gynaikes*)? If they had no political standing in ancient Greek culture, why was one given pride of place at the Games, another allowed to erect a statue of herself as an Olympic victor, and still others given responsibility not only for organizing the Heraea festival but also for keeping peace in their communities? Pausanias himself helps us to answer these questions, showing the important role that women play in the ancient Greek ideals that inspire the Olympic Games—ideals I summarize in my work on Olympic philosophy as humanism, justice, and peace.

Humanism and Heroic *Aretē*

To say that Olympic philosophy is humanistic is to say that it celebrates humanity, more precisely, human excellence (*aretē*). In Ancient Greece, *aretē* was embodied by heroes, and with respect to athletics and the Olympic Games, by Heracles. Not only is Heracles credited in multiple traditions with founding the Olympic Games, his famous *athla* (labors) decorated Olympia's most impressive building, the Temple of Zeus. There is reason to believe that the very concept of "athletics" derives from Heracles's *athla*.

Perhaps this is why Coubertin concluded in his famous speech, "The Philosophic Foundation of Modern Olympism," that "the true Olympic hero is, in my view, the individual adult male." But Coubertin was mistaken, Greek heroes can be male or female, and they are all "athletic" in the sense of performing great feats. Heroic *athla* (and the athletic events that emulate them) are humanistic in that they express a person's *aretē* in distinctively human predicaments or struggles called *agōnes*, like the athletic contests that emulate them.

Since the ancient *Olympiakoi Agōnes* (Olympic Games) emulated, above all, the struggles (*agōnes*) and achievements (*athla*) of Heracles one of the best explanations for the exclusion of *gynaikes* from the Olympic sanctuary during the Games is precisely their link with Heracles, from whose cult married women were routinely excluded.

The religious exclusion of women from Heracles's cult does not, however, entail their exclusion from "athletics" understood as an emulation of Heracles's *athla*. This is because athletics function as a religious/educational evocation of heroic *aretē*, which is not gender-specific; athletes emulate virtues not people. Those who say that there was a separate "women's *aretē*" characterized, for example, by modesty, are confusing gendered people with gender roles. When Pericles sums up "womanly virtue" (*gynaikeias aretēs*) as "not being talked about" (Thucydides 2.45.2), he is referring to the role of wife, which is designated by the same term.

By struggling in a competition that re-enacts some heroic feat, athletes get a feel for heroic *aretē*—an experiential appreciation of what it means to be excellent. The genders of the model emulated and the emulators are irrelevant. For example, the *apobatēs* race at the Panathenaic Games involves male athletes emulating the actions of the female goddess Athena in a mythological battle against the Titans. The context of its expression, not the gender of the agent, determines the type of *aretē* involved. For example, heroic/athletic *aretē* is appropriate in battle, which in Athenian society is performed by men. The *agōn* of childbirth may call for a different expression of *aretē* than the typically masculine *agōn* of battle, but *aretē* itself is neither feminine or masculine, it is human.

It is significant in this context that the goddess Athena is a *parthenos*. Heroic/athletic *aretē* seems to be appropriate to and celebrated by unmarried youth of both sexes. In fact, the most athletic of Greek heroes (male or female) may be a *parthenos* named Atalanta who, in addition to cooperating with male heroes in traditional *athla* like the Calydonian Boar Hunt, became famous for agreeing to marry any man who could outrun her then proceeding to beat them one by one. Her fierce defense of her virginity begins when a pair of Centaurs come to rape her, and she dispatches them with her bow and arrows. This *athlos* connects Atalanta with Heracles, who is said to have killed centaurs in a similar way in a different story.

Part human, part horse, centaurs symbolize the animalistic side of humanity that needs to be put under rational control. Heroic/athletic *aretē* involves the same "taming" or "civilizing" dynamic—for males and females alike. It is no accident that on the western pediment of the Temple of Zeus at Olympia (now on display in Olympia's museum), centaurs are depicted in the act of disrupting a marriage celebration. At the center of the scene is a figure conventionally identified as Apollo (god of reason and order), but who may represent Heracles, holding a bow after triumphantly restoring order to the scene by killing the centaurs just as Atalanta did.

As far as we know Atalanta's image does not appear at Olympia, but the eastern pediment of the Temple of Zeus (also displayed in the museum) features another *parthenos*, Hippodamia, whose name means something like "tamer of horses," and whose heroic *aretē* resulted in order being restored to Olympia's region, the Peloponnese (more on that later). The point here is that the *aretē* cultivated and celebrated in the Olympic Games is not distinctively masculine, but rather distinctively human in that it involves imposing rational order on the uncivilized, animalistic aspects of our nature.

Society may divide according to gender the *contexts* in which *aretē* is typically expressed, but virtue itself is not gendered. In fact, Plato's *Republic* 620b imagines Atalanta's soul choosing to be reincarnated as a male athlete on account of the great honors they receive; the choice makes clear that even exemplary athletic virtue is not a matter of gender. Heroic/athletic *aretē* is humanistic and, as an Olympic ideal, it pertains to males and females alike.

Justice: Separation and Equality

The second key principle of modern Olympic philosophy is justice, understood according to the spirit of sport as equality of opportunity and reward according to merit. It may be justice that scholars find especially lacking in the treatment of women in ancient Olympia. It can hardly be said that men and women enjoyed equal opportunity in ancient athletics—otherwise Atalanta wouldn't have chosen to be reincarnated as a male athlete. But it isn't always clear what equality of opportunity for men and women means in the context of sport.

In Coubertin's essay, "The Philosophic Foundation of Modern Olympism," he says that he thinks women should have the opportunity to engage in sport, just not public competition. Today, the International Olympic Committee pushes for equal numbers of male and female events as well as athletes, but in most sports men and women still compete separately. Does that represent equality of opportunity?

Pausanias says that *parthenoi* competed on the same track but in a separate festival from the men in ancient Olympia:

> Every fourth year there is woven for Hera a robe by the Sixteen women, and the same also hold games called Heraea. The games consist of footraces for maidens [*parthenoi*]. These are not all of the same age. The first to run are the youngest; after them come the next in age, and the last to run are the oldest of the maidens. They run in the following way: their hair hangs down, a tunic reaches to a little above the knee, and they bare the right shoulder as far as the breast. These too have the Olympic stadium reserved for their games, but the course of the stadium is shortened for them by about one-sixth of its length. To the winning maidens they give crowns of olive and a portion of the cow sacrificed to Hera. They may also dedicate statues with their names inscribed upon them. (5.16.2-3)

Bronze figurine in the Heraea costume. 6th century BCE.
© The British Museum, reproduced by license

The shorter length of the race was probably for religious rather than ability reasons, the Temple of Hera at Olympia was likewise one sixth shorter than the Temple of Zeus. In any case, the Heraea must have been a smaller event than the men's Olympic Games, but it is probably just as ancient and at least as significant for the participants involved.

The uniform that Pausanias describes Heraea participants wearing can be seen in artistic images of female athletes that date back to the 6th-century BCE. Most likely, these contests were linked with initiation rituals that marked the transition from childhood to eligibility for marriage—i.e., the status of *parthenos*. Some of the images represent children, probably because some rituals had to be completed before menarche and were only held every four years, but most are young adults—with well-developed breasts and muscles—who appear to have trained seriously for their events.

I think it likely that these races and the training that came before them served to prepare and publicly present potential brides, specifically by showcasing their *aretē* though sport. The men's events may have had a similar origin and function, which would explain why *parthenoi* (i.e., potential brides) were allowed to watch the Games. They might also have been present because the Heraea was held just before or just after the men's festival.

By Pausanias's time in the 2nd century CE, contests for *parthenoi* were part of many major athletic festivals, including the Pythian, Nemean, Isthmian, Sebasta, and Capitoline Games. By then, Olympia may have been conspicuous for the fact that its events for *parthenoi* were still held separately from the men's and retained other characteristics of ancient initiation rituals, such as the costumes Pausanias describes.

For some scholars, the institution of the Heraea and its surrounding events suggests a kind of gender balance in ancient Olympia: Olympic Games organized by men in honor of Zeus complemented by Heraean Games organized by women in honor of his wife, Hera. For others, separate can never be equal, and the fact that ancient female athletes ran shorter distances and were far less famous proves it. Of course, that kind of inequality persists in sport even today, and it should be remembered that in ancient and modern times alike, social roles for men and women differ. Plato, who argues extensively in *Republic* and *Laws* for female participation in sport, does so on the understanding that women will participate in every aspect of political life, including the military, and recognizes that the traditional family structure must be radically altered to accommodate that.

Women's sport in ancient times was apparently linked to preparation for marriage and motherhood. Divine *parthenoi* such as Athena and Artemis remain independent forever, but human *parthenoi* are ultimately expected to become wives. Even the heroic Atalanta eventually succumbed to marriage when the right guy came along—but not before besting dozens of suitors who proved unworthy. It may have been precisely Atalanta's resistance to her suitors that ancient footraces for *parthenoi* were emulating. And at least within their races at Olympia, there was equality of opportunity and reward according to merit (with the same prize as the men).

Peace and Political Agency

Coubertin understood that the ancient Olympic Games served religious ends that facilitated the exclusion of women, but he also paved the way for ancient Greek ideals to serve the modern Movement's political ends, especially peace. What he didn't recognize was women's involvement in those ideals. The modern Olympic truce, for example, was inspired by *ekecheiria,* an ancient decree ensuring safe passage for travelers to Games, which according to Pausanias (5.10.10) was artistically represented as a woman in Olympia's Temple of Zeus. At the ancient Olympic Games, warring parties could safely negotiate peace treaties in an atmosphere that put cultural commonalities above political differences.

Those who assume that women had nothing to do with the peace-promoting functions of the ancient Games need look no further than Pausanias to find them playing a central role. Not only did the *parthenos* Hippodamia bring about political change in the region by means of an athletic contest, but married women also (*gynaikes*) flexed their political muscle by winning Olympic crowns, executing religious and administrative roles, and even negotiating and maintaining peace between Elis and Pisa as they competed for control of the Olympic Games.

Terracotta plaque with Pelops and Hippodamia racing to defeat her father, the tyrant Oenomaus.Roman, 27 BCE–68 CE. Metropolitan Museum of Art number 26.60.32. Open access image.

Hippodamia's story resembles that of Atalanta in that it involves a marriage contest, but in this case, it is a chariot race in which the suitors challenge the bride-to-be's father. King Oenomaus tyrannically "defeated" the first eighteen suitors by killing them with a bow and arrow during the race, then nailed their heads to the columns of his palace. Hippodamia stopped the bloodbath by conspiring with Pelops, her 19th suitor, to sabotage the king's chariot. After Pelops won the race and her hand in marriage, Pausanias tells us, he gave proper burial to her previous suitors (6.2.21), became Olympia's most honored hero (5.1.13), and had the whole Peloponnese named for him.

Hippodamia, too, had a prominent hero's altar in the Olympic sanctuary where married women sacrificed to her, plus a bronze statue in the hippodrome holding a ribbon with which to award her new husband (6.2.20-21). This is all in addition to the Heraean Games which, according to Pausanias, Hippodamia herself inaugurated in gratitude for her wedding with Pelops by organizing the "Sixteen Women" (5.16.4).

The "Sixteen Women" and their assistants, all of whom Pausanias identifies as *gynaikes,* are perhaps the most overlooked exponents of the Olympic value of peace. Says Pausanias (5.16.5-6):

> Besides the account already given they tell another story about the Sixteen Women as follows. Damophon, it is said, when tyrant of Pisa did much grievous harm to the Eleans. But when he died, since the people of Pisa refused to participate as a people in their tyrant's sins, and the Eleans too became quite ready to lay aside their grievances, they chose a woman from each of the sixteen cities of Elis still inhabited at that time to settle their differences, this woman to be the oldest, the most noble, and the most esteemed of all the women. The cities from which they chose the women were Elis, ...The women from these cities made peace between Pisa and Elis. Later on they were entrusted with the management of the Heraean games, and with the weaving of the robe for Hera.

The idea that women are skilled in promoting peace is a part of ancient Greek culture made famous by Aristophanes' comedy *Lysistrata,* in which women stage a sex-strike to force their husbands to end a war. What is significant in this case is its link with the Games at Olympia and the specification that these female peacekeepers were chosen on the basis of public esteem. Clearly the "Sixteen Women" had real political power, which was directly linked with sport.

Not to be overlooked either is the priestess of Demeter Chamyne, whom Pausanias describes as watching the men's Games in the Olympic stadium seated opposite from the *Hellanodikai* on a white altar (which can still be seen onsite today). More than a simple exception to the prohibition against married women at the Games, this position is described as an honor (*timē*) bestowed by the Eleans (6.20.8). Surely, this office was politically prestigious; we know that one of the women who held it was Regilla, the wife of Herodes Atticus, a politically important benefactor of the Olympic Games in Imperial times and sponsor of its elaborate nymphaeum.

Finally, the political ambitions of Cyniska, the first woman to win an Olympic victory (as the owner of racehorses), should be taken seriously. Not only was she a princess of Sparta—a society noted for the athletic education of its girls—Pausanias describes her as *"philotimotata,"* which means something like "exceedingly ambitious for public honor" (3.8.1). He also tells us that she placed votive bronzes of her winning horses inside Olympia's Temple of Zeus (5.12.5), and a statue of herself in the sanctuary, as only victors were allowed to do (6.2.2). According to the *Greek Anthology* 13.16, its inscription read:

> Kings of Sparta were my fathers and brothers, and I, Cyniska, winning the race with my chariot of swift-footed horses, erected this statue. I assert that I am the only woman in all Greece who won this crown.

Pausanias says that in her hometown of Sparta Cyniska was worshipped as a hero (3.15.1), and confirms that after her many more women, especially Spartan women, went on to win Olympic crowns as horse owners (3.8.1).

Conclusion

It is alleged in Plutarch's *Life of Agesilaus* 22 that Cyniska was pushed by her brother to compete at Olympia to prove that victory was a matter of wealth rather than *aretē*; the unexpressed premise being that Greeks believed women couldn't have *aretē*. Another way of looking at it is to say that the Olympic Games provided Cyniska with an opportunity—on equal footing with her male competitors—to publicly demonstrate her *aretē*. In fact, a closer look at Pausanias's text reveals that ancient Olympia provided *parthenoi* and *gynaikes* alike the opportunity to celebrate and perform feats of heroic, athletic, administrative, and diplomatic *aretē*, even though it banned some of them from the sanctuary during the Games.

There is no question that ancient Greek culture can and should be criticized for its historical treatment of women, but we also need to recognize those ancient Greek women who, from within that culture, managed to promote the values of humanism, justice, and peace that underpin the philosophy of the modern Olympic Games. Pierre de Coubertin was philosophically right to say that antiquity cannot be the basis for deciding whether women should participate in the Olympic Games, but he was historically wrong in believing that the only thing they did in ancient Olympia was to crown the male victors. A closer look at their involvement in the myth and history of the Games reveals that women have always been part of ancient Olympic ideals.

The Townley Discobolus, Roman copy of Myron's Greek original.
© The British Museum, reproduced by license.

Beauty:

Kalokagathia: Ethics, Athletics, and Aesthetics

The Ancient Olympic Games are rightly identified as the origin of modern sport, and the ancient Greek gymnasium models its educational use. What is often overlooked in the discussion of ancient sport, however, is its aesthetic aspect. Since sport, art, and philosophy are considered separate in the modern world, we tend to project those divisions onto our study of ancient Greece. This prevents us from seeing the connection between ethics, athletics, and aesthetics that underpins the use of sport as moral education. Fortunately for us, there is a single word that expresses that connection and no less a philosopher than Aristotle discusses it at length. The word is *kalokagathia*, literally "beauty and goodness," and by understanding it, we can better understand sport's potential to function as moral education even today.

Let us begin by imagining Myron's *Discus Thrower*, the most famous of many ancient Greek athletic statues (surviving in the form of Roman copies) offered as illustrations of *kalokagathia*. Invariably, Aristotle's praise of pentathletes' beauty at *Rhetoric* 1361b is cited as evidence for the connection between this statue and *kalokagathia* since the discus throw existed only as part of the pentathlon in ancient athletics. What is important to remember, however, is that *kalokagathia* is not a quality of statues or even bodies; rather it is an ideal of *aretē* (virtue, excellence) *represented* by the athletic image. As I argue elsewhere, the balanced and harmonious beauty of athletic bodies reflects Aristotle's theory of the virtuous soul in *Nicomachean Ethics*.

In *Eudemian Ethics* 8.3, meanwhile, Aristotle characterizes *kalokagathia* as "perfect virtue." But even if we can affirm that Aristotle's ethical ideal of *kalokagathia* is symbolized by athletic art, does it follow that real-life athletes possess *kalokagathia*, or that athletic training contributes to moral development? Furthermore, did the civic identity of being *kalokagathos* have anything to do with athletics or Aristotle's ideal?

Aristotle himself suggests a negative answer to this question at *Politics* 1335b, where he says that "the constitution of an athlete is not suited to the life of a citizen...." But before rejecting outright any link among ethics, athletics, aesthetics and citizenship, we need to understand what *kalokagathia* is and how it might have functioned civically. I think that Aristotle's ideal of *kalokagathia* is compatible not just with athletic training, but also with an ideal of citizenship that rejects traditional ideas about inborn virtue and superficial beauty. *Kalokagathia* results from deliberate character training (*ethos*) complemented by an intellectual understanding of the beautiful (*kalon*). In short, the pentathlete's beauty is a *mimēsis* (representation) of the balanced athletic and humanistic training characteristic of classical Greek gymnasia.

Kalokagathia as a Civic Identity

Classical scholars of the 18th and 19th centuries imagined *kalokagathia* to be a traditional Hellenic ideal with roots buried deep in Homer's epics, early tragedy, and epinician poetry of the kind written by Pindar for victors in the Panhellenic games. In the 20th century, however, a detailed study of the term's use by Bourriot concluded that the term didn't emerge until 5th-century BCE Sparta, where it came to designate men who distinguished themselves in athletics or war. It was later adopted in Athens by a small circle of sophistically trained "snobs" including Alcibiades before becoming a "pet slogan" for the bourgeois elite during the oligarchic revolutions, and eventually evolving into a general term of praise for non-aristocratic elites. Bourriot suggests further that Plato intentionally avoided the term to resist endorsing its political implications, and Aristotle uses it merely to describe the ideal qualities of the leisured class.

Accordingly, when Harris Rackham translated Aristotle's *Eudemian Ethics* around the turn of the 20th century he rendered *kalokagathia* as "nobility," which connotes both social status and moral excellence, and he rendered the personal term *kalokagathos* as "gentleman." One need not deny that *kalokagathia* functioned as a civic identity to affirm that it also designated a meaningful philosophical and educational ideal. But Rackham's translation seems unduly influenced by the aristocratic values of his own age, when European elites were embracing ancient Greek thought as a way of understanding and defending their social status.

As in ancient Greece, the modern aristocracy owed their privilege less to achievement than to wealth and family ties. Translating *kalokagathos* as "gentleman" and *kalos* more generally as "nobility" accordingly suggests a passively inherited state rather than an actively achieved one. But this understanding is at odds with Aristotle's wider ethics and with the understanding of *kalokagathia* as an educational ideal—both of which demand that it be understood as an achievement rather than a birthright. In modern sport, there is a similarly mistaken presumption that athletic excellence is a matter of genetic inheritance. What counts for Aristotle, however, is virtuous *activity*, and that results from training, not birth.

The convention of translating *kalos* as "fine" or "noble" also sidesteps its aesthetic dimension. If *kalokagathia* is nothing more than moral goodness, why not simply call it *agathia*? Why distinguish it at all from *aretē*, the conventional term for virtue? And why *not* translate *kalos* as "beauty"—keeping an open mind about what beauty might mean in this context? Aristotle makes it clear at the outset of his discussion of *kalokagathia* in *Eudemian Ethics* 1248b that "goodness (*agathon*) and *kalokagathia* differ not only in name but also in themselves." And he identifies "goods" as things that "have ends which are to be chosen for their own sake" (1247b).

This description permits not only individual virtues to be good, but also non-moral qualities such as the "natural goods," of honor, wealth, bodily excellences, good fortune, and power. These sorts of things are distinct from moral virtues, but they have in common with *aretē* the fact that they enable their possessor to accomplish worthwhile deeds. Goods and goodness, then, seem to have in common the ability to bring about desirable activity including, but importantly not limited to, athletics. *Kalokagathia*, therefore, cannot be a matter of wealth, rank, honor, or any of the usual qualities that determine social class. It must, like athletic performance, be something realized through activity.

This active understanding of *kalokagathia* is completely consistent with what Aristotle says about virtue (*aretē*) and happiness (*eudaimonia*) in the *Nicomachean Ethics*. There, happiness is said to be "the end of the things achievable in action" (1097b), and human function is identified as "activity of the soul in accord with reason" (1098a). Virtue, furthermore, is what "causes its possessors to be in a good state and to perform their functions well" (1106a). The prize of happiness is achieved not by being in a particular condition, but rather by acting out of that condition. Says Aristotle:

> ...just as Olympic prizes are not for the finest (*kallistoi*) and strongest, but for the contestants—since it is only these who win—the same is true in life; among the fine and good people (*kalōn kagathōn*), only those who act correctly win the prize. (1099a2)

It is noteworthy that Aristotle uses the example of athletes here to prove his point that virtue and happiness depend on performance. Just as an athlete must compete, a *kalokagathos* must act virtuously. Aristotle is not, however, *equating* athletic performance with *kalokagathia*.

If we think of *kalokagathia* in terms of performance, whether or not we follow Rackham in translating it as "nobility," we must not understand it as the passive product of inheritance or social class any more than we think of a champion athlete's performance as the passive result of genetic inheritance. The *kalokagathos* is one who performs good actions, or as Aristotle puts it in the *Eudemian Ethics*, "practices the *kalon*" (1248b). Aristotle says that wealth, high birth, and power are "fitting" for the *kalokagathos* (1249a). But what makes them so is not that he has them by reason of birth or social status; rather it is his ability to use such goods in a beneficial way that makes them appropriate for him.

More precisely, the *kalokagathos'* ability to use natural goods in a beautiful (*kalon*) way is what justifies his possession of them; for it is beauty (*kalon*) which transforms mere goods into the virtuous activity associated not only with *kalokagathia*, but also with *eudaimonia* (happiness). And using goods like strength or wealth beautifully means using them civically, or at least for something other than athletic victory and personal gain. So *kalokagathia* may be a civic identity, but it is not granted at birth; rather it must be earned through beautiful and civically beneficial action.

Kalokagathia as an Educational Ideal

If the quality that makes actions and people beautiful is not a matter of heredity, how exactly is it acquired? Let us look again at Aristotle's praise of athletic beauty in *Rhetoric*:

> For each age there is a different beauty. For a young man, beauty means that one has a body fit for all efforts, both running and the use of strength. He is pleasant to look upon, a pure delight. That is why the pentathletes are the most beautiful people, because they have a natural talent for both strength and swiftness. (1361b)

At first glance, this hardly seems to be the kind of beauty implied by *kalokagathia*. For one thing, the term used here is *kallos* with two lambdas, a kind of beauty associated especially with bodies, rather than *kalos*, a more general term for beauty that encompasses morality and propriety. Secondly, Aristotle seems to be talking about "natural talent" rather than achievement. As the quote continues, however, he goes on to emphasize performance:

> The athletic *aretē* of a body lays in size, strength and swiftness, for who is swift, is also strong. Who is able to throw his legs about in a certain way and move with rapid and large paces, is a good runner. Who can hug and grapple, a wrestler. Who can hit with his fist, a boxer. Who can do both, a pankratiast. Who can do everything, is a pentathlete. (1361b)

Aristotle certainly believes in inherited potential, but he makes it clear that athletic *aretē* depends on ability and action. Likewise, the pentathlete's beauty depends on ability, or more precisely, the development and exercise of his natural potential to the point of reliable performance. Nature, says Aristotle, gives us the capacity for virtue but that capacity must be realized through training (*ethos*) and realized through action. Athletically beautiful activity, then, is not equivalent to morally beautiful activity (i.e., *kalokagathia*), but it is analogous in this way. They both depend on training. What kind of training? The balanced training of thought and action characteristic of the ancient Greek gymnasium.

Athletic training is characterized, as we know, by repetitive actions aimed at perfecting a particular kind of motion. The discus thrower mentioned above achieves his aesthetically pleasing form through practice informed by the instruction of a knowledgeable coach. Likewise, Aristotle says in the *Nicomachean Ethics* that *aretē* is achieved through training (*ethos*) and instruction, adding that it cannot be in us by nature, since nothing natural is altered by training (1103a).

The reason that both training and instruction are required for virtue is that *aretē* encompasses not only character (i.e., the capacity for good and beautiful action), but also intellect (i.e., the understanding of what is good and beautiful). In the discus thrower's case, the coach uses their own understanding of proper form to guide the athlete's training, and it is through repeated action that the athlete him- or herself comes to understand what proper form looks and feels like.

Likewise, in Aristotelian moral education, students begin by performing moral actions and develop, through repeated performance, an understanding of the good and beautiful. As Aristotle puts it in *Nicomachean Ethics* 1103a, we learn ethics (*ēthikē*) from practice (*ethos*), which he takes to be a related word. Some may take issue with my translating *ethos* as training or practice, rather than habit or custom, but Aristotle's description of it is cognate to athletic training and practice: it is the intentional performance of a prescribed action with the educational aim of acquiring facility in performing the action independently.

That facility acquired through training would be *aretē*: virtue, excellence, or as Debra Hawhee fortuitously renders it, "virtuosity." Every athlete experiences the benefit of training and practice. But we need not confuse athletic and moral training to recognize their similarity, and even to speculate that athletic training prepared youth in the gymnasium for the philosophical training that complemented it.

Even if we recognize how athletic and moral training may be related, however, we might not yet see their connection to beauty. Hawhee's "virtuosity" is quite helpful in this context. Acquiring virtues and acting in accordance with them is one thing, but the virtuosic performance of anything implies added aesthetic value. Likewise, in Aristotelian ethics, beauty acts as a morally charged criterion that distinguishes the beautiful-and-good (*kalon kagathon*) from the merely good (*agathon*). Whereas all goods are desirable, he says beautiful (*kala*) goods are not just praiseworthy in themselves but also the *source* of praiseworthy acts (*Eudemian Ethics* 1248b).

Justice and temperance, as the source of just and temperate acts, are given as examples of good and beautiful things in the *Eudemian Ethics*, whereas health and strength are said to be only contingently good because their effects—healthy and vigorous actions—are not necessarily praiseworthy (1248b). Likewise, athletic ability can only be contingently good. "Beautiful goods" such as justice are distinguished from merely ordinary goods such as health in that they reliably produce praiseworthy actions. But what exactly makes things praiseworthy? What, in a word, makes them beautiful?

Again, a connection to the arts is useful since what makes moral actions beautiful for Aristotle seems to be autotelicity, i.e. being an end in itself. Beauty, like art and play, is consistently characterized as something that exists for its own sake and is intrinsically good (rather than as a means to some other end). Likewise, in *Eudemian Ethics,* Aristotle says that

> A man is beautiful and good (*kalokagathos*) because those goods which are beautiful (*kala*) are possessed by him for themselves, and because he practices the beautiful (*kalon*), and for its own sake. (1248b)

He goes on to describe as beautiful (*kala*) "the excellences (*aretai*) and the acts that proceed from excellence (*aretē*)." This echoes what Aristotle says about virtuous action in *Nicomachean Ethics* 1120a, that it is beautiful and done for the sake of beauty. As Aristotle explains in distinguishing the virtue of courage from other conditions that merely resemble it, a courageous person is moved by beauty and not any kind of compulsion (1116a-b).

So, the capacity to be moved by the intrinsic beauty of an action, something understood intellectually, characterizes the *kalokagathos,* and the fact that an action was performed for the sake of beauty is what makes it beautiful. This conclusion does not imply that the physical beauty achieved by pentathletes constitutes *kalokagathia;* it does, however, leave the possibility open that the process of gymnastic training may condition a person's motivations in the appropriate way. Indeed, it is probable that Aristotle connects ethics and athletics because the latter was an important way to cultivate virtues such as self-control (*sophrosynē*), which are useful outside of sport.

But athletic training can only contribute to virtue when it is complemented by an effort to understand what is good and beautiful. It will be remembered that the education traditionally offered in gymnasia, including that promoted by Aristotle's own teacher, Plato, combined *gymnastikē* with *mousikē* (music understood expansively to include art and literature). In the *Republic,* Socrates prescribes this education for the ideal city's future leaders, emphasizing that the two must work together to harmonize the students' souls:

> ...a god has given music and physical training to human beings not, except incidentally for the body and the soul, but for the spirited and wisdom-loving parts of the soul itself, in order that these may be in harmony with one another, each being stretched and relaxed to an appropriate degree. (*Republic* 411e-412a)

Mousikē is often equated with modern humanities, which in ancient times most often took the form of poetry, but also included singing, instrumental music, and even dance, in which bodily motion is guided by beautiful music. This function matches well with what Aristotle designates as the intellectual aspect of moral education because it helps the student to acquire a sense of the beautiful and good.

79

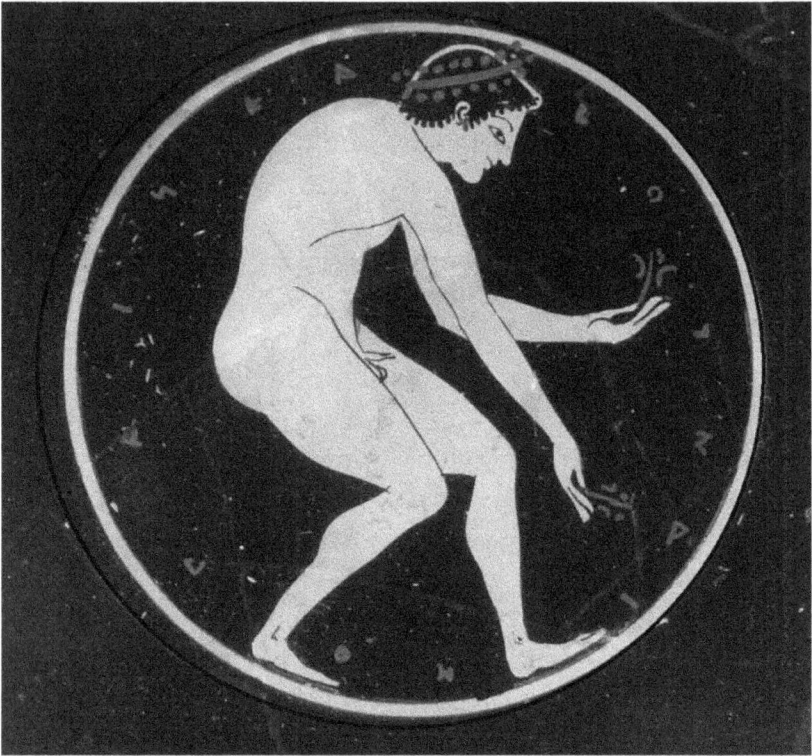

Kylix inscribed "Ho pais kalos" (the beautiful youth), ca. 510 BCE. Metropolitan Museum of Art, number 09.221.47. Open access image.

Gymnastikē, meanwhile, which includes athletic contests, is used not only as physical training but also to test potential leaders for the ability to promote the city's interests despite the temptations of pleasure and compulsion of pain. How this all works is the subject of another project but suffice it to say that the kind of discernment expected of Plato's philosopher kings as a result of their education in gymnastics and music is very close to the discernment expected of Aristotle's *kalokagathos*.

Kalokagathia as a civic ideal

The discernment of moral beauty functions as a civic ideal because it requires the *kalokagathos* to transcend partisan interests and act, so to speak, for a greater good. Aristotle claims in *Eudemian Ethics* 1249a that people lacking *kalokagathia* fail to distinguish between what is expedient and what is intrinsically good. As a result, they mistakenly regard things like honor, wealth and power as good in themselves, while viewing intrinsic goods like justice merely as means to those lesser goods.

Likewise within sport, we criticize athletes who do whatever it takes to win, who play only for the money, or act selfishly on the field. On the other hand, we celebrate people like Bill Bradley, who transferred the values he gained playing professional basketball into a respected career as a United States Senator. Spectators, too, are morally criticized for partisanship, and praised for the ability to rise above it and appreciate sport as a spectacle of beauty.

I describe this characteristic *of kalokagathia* as discernment, i.e., of seeing things a certain way, because a key part of virtue in the *Nicomachean Ethics* is precisely the ability to discern beautiful (*kalon*) ends (1094a, 1155b). This understanding is consistent with Plato's idea of *aretē* as knowledge of the good and his denial of *akrasia* (weakness of will), which holds that humans never act against what we believe to be good—we just make intellectual mistakes about what is really good.

On Aristotle's scheme, such people may have virtues, but they do not have *kalokagathia*,

> ...for it is not true of them that they acquire the noble (*kalon*) for itself, that they choose acts good and noble at once.... (*Eudemian Ethics* 1249a3-4)

To put it another way, they fail to reliably recognize the beauty of the good. It is again clear from this that athletic ability is not to be equated with *kalokagathia* or even virtue. It is, however, an athlete's virtue that enables her to direct that athletic ability toward the good—whether it be a beautiful good such as justice, or a lesser good like glory or gain

Aristotle describes this instrumental use of virtue as a disposition characteristic of the Spartans. In ancient athletics, Spartans were famous for declaring "victory or death" and refusing to concede in wrestling and *pankration*—in one case to the point of death. This may have been honorable, but it was not beautiful as long as it was motivated by the desire for glory or the fear of disgrace—both of which are forms of compulsion.

"The man who thinks he ought to have excellences for the sake of external goods," says Aristotle at *Eudemian Ethics* 1249b, "does deeds that are *kala* only *per accidens*." Further, natural goods such as honor, wealth, physical excellence, and good fortune may be harmful to people lacking discernment of the greater good (1248a):

> For neither the foolish nor the unjust nor the intemperate would get any good from the employment of them, any more than an invalid from the food of a healthy man, or one weak and maimed from the equipment of one in health and sound in all limbs.

It takes discernment to turn natural goods (including athletic ability) into truly praiseworthy actions. For the *kalokagathos*, says Aristotle (1249a):

> things profitable are also beautiful (*kala*), but to the many, the profitable and the beautiful (*kala*) do not coincide, for things absolutely good are not good for them as they are for the good man; to the *kalokagathos* they are also beautiful (*kala*).

There seem to be three levels here. First, there are the masses (*hoi polloi*), for whom goods like wealth and power may actually be a disadvantage—as when winning the lottery ruins a person's life, or turning a star player into a coach ruins the team's performance. Second there is the *agathos*, for whom good things are advantageous but not (except by accident) beautiful. And finally there is the *kalokagathos,* for whom good things are advantageous and also beautiful because, as Aristotle explains, "he does many beautiful (*kala*) deeds by reason of them" (1249a).

What *kalokagathia* does is put the virtues in the service of a higher good—something like Plato's form of the good, which is intimately connected to beauty. Athletes dedicated to their sport—which is neither good nor bad—often have little time to serve the higher good. But complete dedication to sport should not last a lifetime; the virtues cultivated through sport fulfill their purpose only when they are used to perform beautiful actions beyond it. Knowing what ends to pursue with one's virtue is at least as important as having the virtue itself.

Aristotle suggests in *Eudemian Ethics* 1249a6 that the *kalokagathos'* autotelic choice—choosing the beautiful for the sake of beauty—is what *makes* things beautiful:

> For objects are beautiful (*kala*) when a man's motives
> for acting and choosing them are beautiful (*kala*).

This idea is echoed in the Roman Imperial period by the orator Dio Chrysostom, who blames the demise of athletic beauty in his day on the lack of people who appreciate it: "When [beauty] is disregarded and esteemed by no one, or when wicked men esteem it, it fades away like reflections in a mirror" (71.2). What is naturally good, says Aristotle, appears beautiful to the *kalokagathos* (*Eudemian Ethics* 1249a).

At this point, however, it seems like we are running in circles. An end is beautiful when it is chosen for the sake of beauty, and it is chosen for the sake of beauty because it is beautiful. A person is beautiful and good, furthermore, because he chooses goods for the sake of beauty, and goods become beautiful because the person who chooses them is beautiful and good.

Aristotle attempts to untangle this knot in *Eudemian Ethics* 1249a using the civic example of justice:

> For what is just is beautiful (*kalon*), justice is in proportion to merit, and he merits these things; or what is fitting is beautiful (*kalon*), and to him these things — wealth, high birth, and power — are fitting.

The distinguishing point here seems to be that the *kalokagathos* understands justice not like the *Republic*'s Thrasymachus as the worldly interest of the stronger, but rather according to an ideal of proportion or measure according to merit. That is to say, he sees the *beauty* of justice and chooses it for that reason rather than as a means to personal or political benefit.

For the same reason, the social advantages of wealth, high birth, and power befit the *kalokagathos* because he will not use these things simply to benefit himself but rather put them into the service of higher ideals and the wider community. With all the modern handwringing over big salaries being paid to star athletes, an education in how to direct those assets toward the good seems appropriate.

Conclusion

At this point we can affirm that *kalokagathia* is a robust ethical ideal that transcends mere social class and runs deeper than the superficial beauty of athletic bodies. Like athletic excellence, it is the result of training and instruction, rather than natural talent or even natural goods. Furthermore, it results in beautiful actions — although morally beautiful actions and athletically beautiful actions are not identical.

The integrated education found in Greek gymnasia seeks to cultivate moral discernment by simultaneously stimulating an understanding of the good and beautiful, while prescribing repeated actions in accordance with those ideals. And since, as Plato argued in the *Republic*, such integrated education will result in some leaders capable of transcending personal interests and acting strictly for the greater good (philosopher kings had neither personal property nor nuclear families), the *kalokagathos* can represent a civic ideal, though not a civic identity assigned on the basis of external criteria. Insofar as athletic training helps to prepare an individual for achieving *kalokagathia* it should certainly be encouraged, even today.

So why in *Politics* 1335b does Aristotle reject the idea that professional athletes would make good citizens? He explains that it is because "their labor is excessive or of one sort only." He, unlike we so often do, has not confused the professional athlete with the youth trained for citizenship in the gymnasium. He, unlike we, has not assumed that athletic training engages only the body. And he, unlike we, has acknowledged the importance of beauty in moral education.

Aristotle's active, aesthetic, and autotelic understanding of *kalokagathia* is actually the logical (though rarely achieved) goal of gymnasia like Plato's Academy and his own Lyceum. And though *kalokagathia* is an end in itself, it rewards its practitioner with pleasure—the special kind of pleasure that supervenes upon virtuous and beautiful activity. As Aristotle concludes in *Eudemian Ethics* 1249a:

> The absolutely pleasant is also beautiful (*kala*) and the absolutely good (*agatha*) is also pleasant. But pleasure only arises in action; therefore the truly happy man will also live most pleasantly: that this should be is no idle demand of man.

Nor should it be an idle demand of us to better understand the connection between ethics, athletics, and aesthetics.

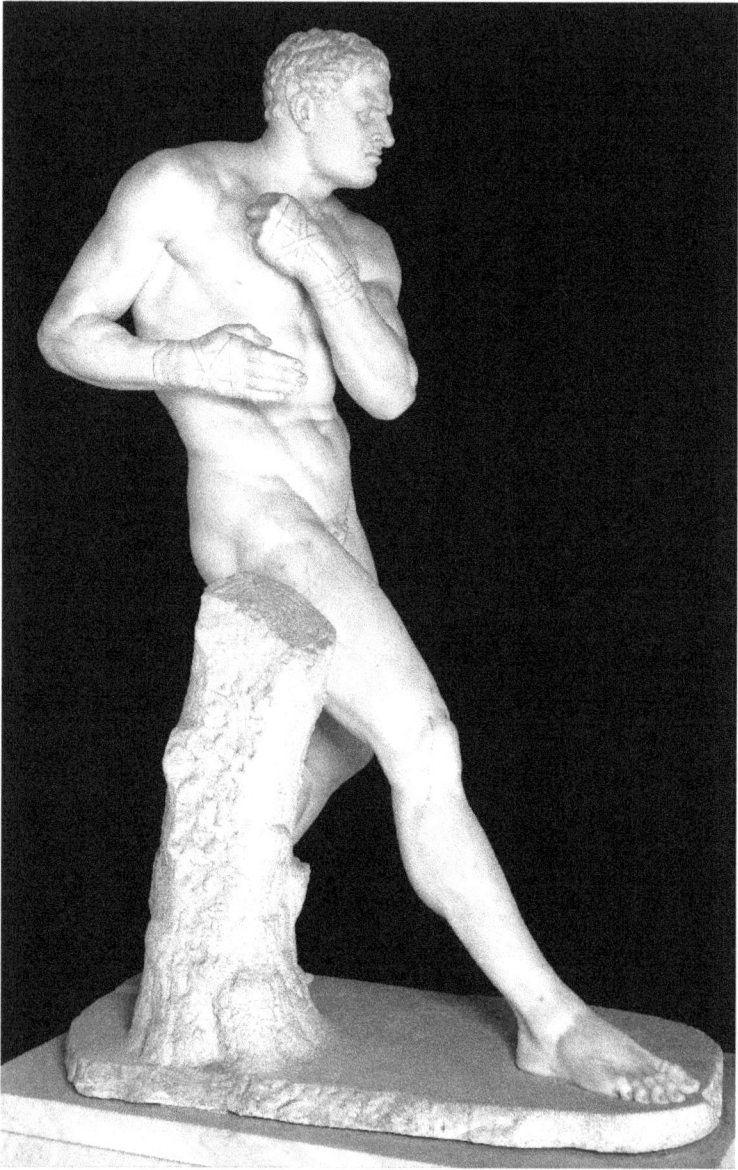

Damoxenos by Antonio Canova (1757-1822)
Musei Vaticani, Museo Pio-Clementino. Photo Copyright © Governorate of
the Vatican City State - Directorate of the Vatican Museums.

Fairness:

Aristotle on the Beauty of Fair Play

The English epithet "fair" is used today almost exclusively to express ethical ideas about impartiality and just distribution of goods. This is particularly true in philosophy, where John Rawls' characterization of justice as fairness in *A Theory of Justice* expresses an analytic understanding of the concept almost completely detached from the aesthetic dimension of that word. In sport, too, the ideal of fair play is understood primarily in terms of rule-adherence and principles such as equal opportunity. But since we critically apply the epithet "fair" to rules and principles themselves, understanding fairness demands an appeal to some concept beyond rules and principles. In fact, rules, principles, and their applications may be said to derive from a pre-existing ideal of fairness—an ideal that has an important aesthetic dimension.

Let me illustrate with an ancient example. Pausanias (8.40.4-5) tells the story of an ugly boxing match at the Nemean Games in which Damoxenos of Syracuse killed Kreugas of Epidamnos after they agreed to settle the contest by allowing each to land one undefended blow. Damoxenos struck Kreugas with his fingers outstretched, piercing the skin with his fingernails and pulling out Kreugas' intestines. This was not explicitly against the rules, but the judges awarded the victory to Kreugas posthumously, ruling that the five-fingered strike amounted to multiple blows.

The judges' explanation for their decision was dubious, but their appeal to fairness was clear, and I think they were appealing—at least in part—to an ideal of ethical beauty, *to kalon* in ancient Greek, which was recognized by Plato and Aristotle both as an important moral quality applicable to agents, motivations, actions, and outcomes. *Kalon* is sometimes translated as "beautiful", but in ethical contexts it is more often rendered as "fine," "noble," or "honorable." I believe that if we think of Aristotle's *kalon* as an ethical aesthetic akin to fairness, we not only achieve a better understanding of the connection between beauty and goodness that informs his ethics, we also achieve a richer and less analytical understanding of fairness and fair play as ethical concepts applied in (and perhaps derived from) sport.

Fairness vs. Justice

Fairness for Aristotle is a disposition, specifically the disposition of the *kalokagathos*, the good and beautiful person. As a disposition that produces good action it is a kind of *aretē* (virtue or excellence), but one distinct from more conventional virtues such as courage, piety, self-control and so on. In the *Eudemian Ethics*, Aristotle calls *kalokagathia* the excellence that arises from a combination of excellences and concludes that it is *aretē teleios* (perfect excellence). What distinguishes the good and beautiful person from the merely good person, he says at 1248b, is the source and end of their actions:

> Now being good and being fair (*kalon kagathon*) are really different not only in their names but also in themselves. For all goods have Ends that are desirable in and for themselves. Of these, all those are fair (*kalon*) which are laudable as existing for their own sakes, for these are the Ends which are both the motives of laudable actions and laudable themselves —justice itself and its actions, and temperate actions, for temperance also is laudable; but health is not laudable, for its effect is not, nor is vigorous action laudable, for strength is not—these things are good but they are not laudable.

If a fair person is one who performs fair actions, then this person's motives as well as their ends will be not only beautiful but the beautiful (*to kalon*) itself.

What seems to distinguish the disposition of fairness from other virtues, then, is the ability to ascertain what is morally beautiful. Aristotle argues that such ascertainment is not merely a matter of theoretical knowledge but a specific kind of knowledge capable of producing the appropriate actions:

> Although it is fair (*kalon*) even to attain a knowledge of the various beautiful things, all the same nevertheless in the case of *aretē* it is not the knowledge of its essential nature that is most valuable but the ascertainment of the sources that produce it. For our aim is not to know what courage is but to be courageous, not to know what justice is but to be just, in the same way as we want to be healthy rather than to ascertain what health is, and to be in good condition of body rather than to ascertain what good bodily condition is. (*Eudemian Ethics* 1216b).

The *kalokagathos*, then, not only must have an understanding of the beautiful, he or she must have the ability to apply that understanding to particular situations in such a way as to discern and perform the fairest course of action.

This is consistent with Aristotle's standard distinction between theoretical and practical wisdom, the combination of which gets us to virtue. What fairness does is to add an aesthetic dimension to morality that elevates *kalokagathia* above mere virtue. The *kalokagathos* is able to recognize beautiful qualities such as order, proportion, and definition within actions and judges them accordingly. Fairness, then, is a virtue of discernment that not only allows the agent to choose fair actions, but also enables him or her to discern when actions are not fair, even if they conform technically to analytic standards of justice. This is what the judges of the Nemean Games did when they disqualified Kreugas for killing his opponent, even though had not technically broken any rules.

Fair Beginnings

Aristotelian fairness requires not only that we discern what is fair but also that we *act out of* fairness. In *Nicomachean Ethics* 1116b, Aristotle is clear that *aretē* requires us to be "moved by *to kalon* and not compulsion." Compulsion in this context refers not just to external demands, but also to irrational internal factors such as strong emotions or appetites. How many fans have their sense of fairness skewed by a strong desire to win? They praise officials only if it benefits their team. Officials, by contrast, are expected to be purely rational.

As with Plato before him and many philosophers since, Aristotle understood virtue largely as being guided by reason or intellect (*logos*). But we should not have too analytic an understanding of *logos*, for it is also through *logos* that we get to beauty. As he says in *Eudemian Ethics* 1229a:

> For courage is following *logos*, and *logos* bids us to choose what is fair (*kalon*). Hence he who endures formidable things not on account of *logos* is either out of his mind or daring, but only he who does so from motives of fairness (*kalon*) is fearless and brave.

Virtuous action including fair play comes about through *logos*, then, but *logos* is not limited to rational calculation, it is also the faculty which discerns beauty. Fair play must furthermore be voluntary—a matter of self-governance by *logos* rather than external compulsion such as the fear of punishment, or internal compulsion from emotions or appetites such as greed.

To say that fairness has its origin in beauty is not to exclude rational characteristics such as rule-adherence or impartiality from it—but it does suggest that fairness cannot be reduced to them. In fact, as our Nemean games example and the continuing *practice* of sport shows very well, fairness is a concept that transcends rules and depends on a deeper understanding of the values intrinsic to sport—otherwise we would have no basis from which to evaluate the fairness of the rules. What we need is a richer, more aesthetic sense of fairness capable, if you will, of *sensing* justice rather than calculating it.

It is no coincidence that the discipline of aesthetics tells us that art is also something voluntary, characterized by its ability to engage higher intellectual capacities. The characteristics of beauty Aristotle lists at *Metaphysics* 1078a: order, symmetry, and definition, are found not just in classical works of art, but also in ethical concepts like fair play. In fact, Aristotle's own concept of justice is underpinned by order, symmetry, and definition—the very concepts he associates with beauty. One can also see him thinking aesthetically when he says at *Eudemian Ethics* 1238b that

> the man worthy of small things but claiming great
> ones is blameworthy, for it is foolish and not *kalon* to
> obtain what does not correspond to one's deserts.

Being able to judge whether competitive opportunities are equal and winners are deserving would depend in Aristotle's ethics on an appeal to aesthetic concepts.

Ontologically, this is to say that beauty and goodness are the origin and source (*archē*) of ethical action. At *Metaphysics* 1013a, Aristotle declares that, "the good and the beautiful are the origin both of knowledge and of the movement of many things," and he argues—against the Pythagoreans—that perfect beauty and goodness must have existed from the start since otherwise they would be perfect causes of the less perfect goodness and beauty found in the world.

So first, perfect beauty exists as an unchanging ideal, then individual minds come to know it more or less well through its imperfect instantiations in the world. This understanding of *to kalon*, in turn, inspires the *kalokagathos* not only to discern but also to perform actions in the world which approximate that ideal of as closely as possible.

In sport, we may imagine a diver tapping into her understanding of order, symmetry, and definition to execute a beautiful dive, then a judge would tap into his understanding of the same ideals in order to recognize and evaluate the beauty of the dive. But we need not limit ourselves to the so-called "aesthetic" sports to see how such a dynamic works. The football player, too, taps into an idea of fairness when deciding whether to kick the ball out of bounds so an apparently injured player can receive medical care. The referee appeals to the same idea of fairness in discerning when and whether to call fouls. Though the specific conception of football fair play is distinct from the generalized ideal of Fairness that underpins all ethical action, this ideal is still the origin of that conception and the ultimate origin of all good and beautiful actions.

Fair Ends

The ideal of *kalon* is not only the beginning of fair play; it must also be its end. In the *Nicomachean Ethics* 1120a Aristotle describes virtuous actions as not only beautiful in themselves but also done for the sake of beauty. On the face of it, this seems circular and indeed fairness may be described as something *autotelic*—an end in itself. Autotelicity is characteristic of sport, art, and their common ancestor, play.

By making autotelicity characteristic of fairness, Aristotle may seem to be suggesting that ethics is a form of play, but really he is just emphasizing its aesthetic dimension and distinguishing the merely good action from the truly virtuous one—or to put it in terms of agents, distinguishing the merely *agathos* from the *kalokagathos*.

Aristotle holds that all goodness involves choice, and that "goodness makes a man choose everything for the sake of some object, and that object is what is *kalon*" (*Eudemian Ethics* 1230a). But sometimes agents do a poor job distinguishing the truly beautiful end from the only apparently beautiful one, or from an end that appears beautiful for the wrong reasons.

An official with a rhabdos (switch) and another competitor observe a pankration contest. Terracotta skyphos attributed to the Theseus Painter, ca. 500 BCE. Metropolitan Museum of Art number: 06.1021.49. Open access image.

A common cause of mistaken beauty is the opposite of autotelicity: instrumentalism, i.e., valuing something merely as a means to some end. In *Problems* Aristotle illustrates this by showing how things may appear "beautiful in a view of certain use" without being beautiful in themselves—as when sexual desire causes someone who is appropriate for that activity to appear beautiful. But he argues that the existence of true beauty is "proved by the fact that even grown men appear to us beautiful, when we look at them without any idea of sexual intercourse" (896b).

What the *kalokagathos* aims for, and what he puts his virtues in the service of, must be beauty in and of itself. People lacking *kalokagathia* may still have virtues, explains Aristotle in *Eudemian Ethics* 1248b-1249a, but insofar as they use their virtues as means to acquire other goods such as wealth, honor, power, or sexual pleasure, they are not beautiful (*kalon*).

Here we may seem to have departed from common sporting ideas about fair play. An athlete who plays sport as a means to such ends as "wealth, health, honor, and power" need not be playing unfairly. What we are usually worried about in sport is that focus on external ends leads to an overemphasis on winning, which leads to attempts to secure unfair advantages through cheating, deception, doping, and so on. The existence of external rewards and indeed the effort to win seem completely consistent with fair play as long as athletes respect the rules and spirit of the game.

The Aristotelian question would be *why*, or perhaps *how* does the athlete respect the rules and spirit of the game? Is it because such respect makes activity itself possible or is it because the desired external rewards are available only to those who show such respect? Clearly the latter attitude is characteristic of the educational use of sport—we try and construct games that reward virtues as an incentive to cultivate those virtues. But once an athlete actually has *aretē*, she should play fairly and autotelically—out of respect for the game itself—and not for any further purpose.

Says Aristotle, "the man who thinks he ought to have excellences (*aretai*) for the sake of external goods, does deeds that are fair (*kalon*) only accidentally" (*Eudemian Ethics* 1249a). He illustrates with the example of courage:

> Courage being a form of goodness will make a man face formidable things for some object, so that he does not do it through ignorance (for it rather makes him judge correctly), nor yet for pleasure, but because it is fair (*kalon*), since in a case where it is not fair (*kalon*) but insane he will not face them, for then it would be shameful to do so. (*Eudemian Ethics* 3.1230a)

So courage is only fair if it is exercised for the sake of fairness, just as all virtuous actions are made *kalon* by their ends. This seems consistent with fair play—shaking hands after a game is only fair play if it is done out of respect for one's opponent. Fair play is only fair if it is chosen for the sake of fairness.

Fair Rewards

If Aristotle's high standards seem to be taking all the fun out of fairness, think again. Pleasure should not be the end for the sake of which fair acts are undertaken, but the *kalokagathos* does get pleasure from performing fair actions precisely because she recognizes their beauty. Furthermore because she recognizes fairness, she uses goods fairly and therefore creates additional fair and beautiful things. One way Aristotle distinguishes the *kalokagathos* from others is by the fact that natural goods are good for him, unlike for vicious people. Says Aristotle (*Eudemian Ethics* 1249a):

> For things are fair (*kala*) when that for which men do them and choose them is fair (*kala*). Therefore to the fair (*kalos*) man the things good by nature are fair (*kala*); for what is just is fair (*kalon*), and what is according to worth is just, and he is worthy of these things; and what is befitting is fair (*kalon*), and these things befit him—wealth, birth, power. Hence for the fair (*kalos*) man the same things are both advantageous and fair (*kala*); but for the multitude these things do not coincide, for things absolutely good are not also good for them, whereas they are good for the good man; and to the fair (*kalos*) man they are also fair (*kala*), for he performs many fair (*kala*) actions because of them.

Again there is a kind of a virtuous circle here. The fair man rejects the expedient in favor of the fair, which he chooses for the sake of fairness, and this fairness becomes expedient for him because he is fair. This formula reminds me of an Italian cyclist named Paolo Salvodelli who was renowned for his sense of fair play—for example, he would not attack riders who had crashed or had mechanical problems even when doing so would have been to his competitive advantage. Because of this he was respected in the peloton and competitors generally refrained from attacking him under similar circumstances— which was an advantage for him. But if gaining this advantage would have been his original end, he never would have gained it in the first place. The benefits of fairness, including pleasure, supervene on the autotelic nature of fair actions.

Fairness is not only pleasant, it may even be seen as a form of self-love. In his discussion of the topic in *Nicomachean Ethics*, Aristotle distinguishes the vice of selfishness from the virtue of self-love in terms of beauty. He says, "We censure those who put themselves first" but recognize that a good man acts "from a sense of what is fair (*kalon*)" and expect him to put his friend's interests first, "disregarding his own" (1168a). Yet Aristotle denies at 1169a that acting out of beauty disregards the self:

> The good man will be a lover of self in the fullest degree [because] if all men vied with each other in moral fairness and strove to perform the fairest deeds, the common welfare would be fully realized, while individuals also could enjoy the greatest of goods, inasmuch as virtue is the greatest good.

Aristotle then goes so far as to describe the pleasure that supervenes on fairness as "rapture," pointing out that a virtuous man will give up all his worldly goods, including wealth, power, and even his life,

> ...if he can secure fairness (*to kalon*) for himself; since he would prefer an hour of rapture to a long period of mild enjoyment, a year of [*kalon*] life to many years of ordinary existence, one great and glorious exploit to many small successes. (*Nicomachean Ethics* 1169a)

One is reminded here of the ethos of heroes, especially Achilles who chooses glory over immortality. Indeed ancient athletics may be a reenactment of the virtues of the heroes, as explained in chapter two. The athlete who reenacts heroic virtues benefits not only his community, but also himself since virtues are goods. But athletes wont acquire virtue through sports if they plays them simply as a means to ends like glory and gain.

Conclusion

Aristotelian ethics is rightly said to aim at happiness (*eudaimonia*), which is understood as activity in accordance with virtue. We must not underestimate the role of beauty in that process, however, and we should recognize happiness as something aesthetic as well as ethical—something akin to fairness. In describing *to kalon* in the *Rhetoric*, Aristotle says,

> Fairness, then, is that which, being desirable in itself is at the same time worthy of praise, or which, being good, is pleasant because it is good. If this is fairness (*to kalon*), then virtue must of necessity be fair (*kalon*), for, being good, it is worthy of praise. (1366a)

We have seen that *to kalon* in Aristotle is a concept quite relevant to the athletic concept of fair play, which requires that actions be performed out of sense of fairness and for the end of fairness. This is to say that we should play fairly for sport's own sake, or out of respect for the game, and we should strive to achieve an understanding of the activity's intrinsic beauty as embodied in the spirit of the game. This striving for fairness in sport should be complemented by an appreciation of and pursuit of fairness in life. The path to happiness may be steep and demand virtue but is also beautiful and pleasant. As Aristotle concludes at *Eudemian Ethics* 1214a:

> Happiness (*eudaimonia*) is at once the pleasantest and the fairest (*kallistos*) and best of all things whatever.

Terracotta bobbin with Nike awarding a victorious athlete.
Attributed to the Penthesilea Painter, ca. 460–450 BCE
Metropolitan Museum of Art number: 28.167.
Open access image.

Peace:

Olympic Sport and Its Lessons for Peace

To the ancient Greeks, an Olympic victory was imagined as a visit from the winged goddess *Nikē*, who swooped down from Olympus to briefly bless the mortal athlete with a divine crown of sacred olive. To us moderns, Olympic victory is more likely to be associated with Nike, the multinational megacompany, which swoops down from Wall Street to briefly bless the athlete with a fat paycheck and temporary status as a corporate shill. Just as the corporate Nike differs from the goddess after whom it is named, the modern Olympic Games differ in important ways from their ancient ancestor.

The Olympic Movement should nevertheless take its ancient inspiration seriously. After all, the ancient festival boasts a rarely interrupted millennium-long history, while the modern Games have already been stopped twice by war in the relative infancy of their first century. For a movement that proclaims one of its central goals to be peace, that does not seem to be the most auspicious of beginnings. Do the ancients have any lessons to teach us moderns about the relationship between sport and peace? Or is the Olympic ideal of peace, like the ancient goddess *Nikē*, merely a rhetorically convenient marketing tool to be exploited for power and profit?

I believe that we can learn from the ancient association between the Olympic Games and peace because that association derives not merely from mythology and rhetoric but also from the specific (and perhaps unexpected) effects of athletic competition itself. I think that Olympic sport *taught* the ancient Hellenes something about peace by obliging them to set aside their conflicts, treat others as equals, and tolerate differences. These aspects of Olympic sport derive partly from cultural particularities in ancient Greece, but they continue to manifest themselves in the structure of the modern Games.

As such, the Olympic Games retain the potential to teach us similar lessons — as long as we are willing to listen. This requires us to do more than recount what our predecessors *did* — it demands that we ask *why* they did it and that we seek common ground between their reasons and ours. The goal of this essay is to discover enlightening intersections in the relationship among Ancient Greek culture, Olympic sport, and the philosophical ideal of peace that emerged at the onset of the modern age. It seeks to revive the lessons inherent in the Olympic tradition so that they may continue to help us in the struggle for peace.

Olympic Peace: An Ancient Paradox

The ideal of Olympic peace is paradoxical — typical of the Delphic Oracle that is said to have proposed it. What on earth makes anyone think that international peace and goodwill can be promoted through competition among national teams? Although the Olympic Charter states explicitly that the Olympic Games are competitions between athletes and not among countries, there is no denying that the Games provide a stage for the expression of international rivalry and conflict, which potentially breeds nationalism and divisiveness.

Some would say that the Olympic Movement should remove all pretense of promoting peace and admit its status as a sports-entertainment product that profits by manipulating nationalistic emotions and staging mock battles among political foes. As a political tool, the Olympic Games have at best a checkered past. There is no denying that if peace is an Olympic goal, the Games have fallen short of the mark in both ancient and modern times. Of all the Olympic ideals inherited from the ancients, peace is perhaps the most puzzling.

Ancient Greece itself was hardly a beacon of peace and concord. Their society was at least as warlike as ours, and the Olympic Games featured cultural and political rivalries just as bitter as those seen today. Contests between Spartans and

Athenians, between mainland Greeks and those hailing from Sicily or Asia Minor, were no doubt as emotionally charged as modern battles between China and Taiwan, or Israel and Iran. Political rivalries certainly compromised contests on occasion in antiquity, as they do today. And there is no denying that the sanctuary at Olympia was filled with dedications of weapons and armor: thanks to Zeus for success in war. As Nigel Crowther observes, ancient visitors witnessing all those martial dedications would be much more likely to correlate Olympia with war rather than peace.

Nonetheless, the ancient Olympic festival somehow developed an association with peace. The promotion of friendship and unity among the Greeks was explicitly identified as the reason that the hero Heracles founded, and the king Iphitos revived the Olympic Games. Although such mythology better reflects the wishes of its creators than historical reality, it can be concluded from the existence of these myths that the peace association was at some point taken seriously, even if it was not the historical reason for the inauguration of the Games.

The historical record suggests that Olympia's association with peace grew stronger as the Games matured. Famous orators including Gorgias, Lysias, and Isocrates preached Panhellenism (i.e. unity among often warring Greek tribes) to festival crowds, Olympic officials were used as ambassadors of peace, and there is evidence of a court being set up at Olympia to mediate disputes among Greek city-states. Although the ancient Games clearly failed to eradicate war and enmity, they tirelessly declared their truce and brought diverse people together to engage in rule-governed, nonviolent struggle. The Games' ability to promote an atmosphere of friendship and solidarity among otherwise diverse (and often warring) peoples may indeed be their most remarkable (and perhaps unexpected) legacy.

The athletic contests at Olympia were primarily intended for the religious purpose of attracting pilgrims and (especially) the attention of the gods. The effects of such gatherings transcended religion, however, and apparently resulted in feelings of community and solidarity among those gathered, not unlike today's Olympic Games. Athletes were supported, rewarded, and cheered on by their particular city-states, but the overall emphasis at Olympia was on everyone's common Hellenicity. To go to Olympia was, in some sense, to be Greek

Most likely it was the atmosphere and attitudes created by the religious sports festival that generated the Olympics' association with peace, as well as the pacifist myths about its origins. Notably, our sources for these myths come centuries after the Olympic Games began; Pindar writes around the 5th century BCE and Pausanias writes in the 2nd century C.E. The drive for Hellenic unity was especially strong around the time of the Persian Wars (500–449 BCE). Peaceful reconciliation was also a popular theme for Olympic orations during the Peloponnesian War (431–404 BCE).

The association between the Olympic Games and peace was made explicit in the modern Olympic Charter. Its "Fundamental Principles of Olympism," identify the promotion of "a peaceful society" as one of its primary goals. Furthermore, part of the "Mission and Role of the IOC" is

> ...to cooperate with the competent public or private organizations and authorities in the endeavor to place sport at the service of humanity and thereby to promote peace.

These are vague assertions that leave little guidance by way of method. A clue might be derived, however, from the fourth Fundamental Principle's definition of "Olympic spirit" as mutual understanding, friendship, solidarity, and fair play. Perhaps this is where Olympism and pacifism meet, since these qualities are linked not just with the practice of sport but also with the philosophies of peace that emerge in the modern age.

A closer look at this relationship reveals that Olympic-style sport can cultivate peaceful attitudes in three ways: first, by carving out space and time for putting aside conflicts (truce and sanctuary); second, by treating individuals as equals under the rules of the game (equality and fair play); and third, by tolerating and even celebrating differences (solidarity and mutual understanding). The Olympic Movement's most valuable contribution to peace comes at the grassroots level — the conscious cultivation of peaceful attitudes through the image of its festival and the playing of its games.

Truce and Sanctuary

The first lesson that the Olympic Games can teach us about peace is that a time and place have to be set aside for it. Philosophers disagree about whether peace is a natural state for humanity. Thomas Hobbes famously declared mankind's natural state to be one of warring enemies in a world dominated by "scarcity and fear." The Renaissance Christian Erasmus countered that every sort of being has an innate sense of peace and concord. In the ancient Greek tradition, Hesiod declared strife to be the basis of human life itself, but he distinguished the good strife that motivates competition from the bad strife that fosters war. He also evoked a mythical Golden Age (succeeded in Olympic style by Silver and Bronze Ages) during which humanity thrived without war.

We all seek that Golden Age of peace and thriving, recognizing it as a higher expression of our humanity than war and enmity. Because such a condition is rarely part of our daily lives, deliberate efforts at peace have to be made. We must intentionally carve out times and places where conflict is set aside in order to achieve this higher purpose. So far, so good, but how did athletic contests become that kind of place?

The initial answer is a religious one. Ancient Greek religious sanctuaries were considered the property of the gods, specifically marked off from the realm daily life. Sanctuaries hosted sacrificial rituals in which divine favor was exchanged for some kind of gift. The success of such exchanges depended on attracting the gods' attention. Perhaps it was for this reason that athletic games were at some point added to the sacrificial ritual at Olympia—such a spectacle would attract the attention of gods and mortals alike.

Like every other religious ritual, the Olympic Games were separate from worldly concerns and conflict. The Olympic sanctuary was a special place in which diverse peoples, who might otherwise be strangers or even enemies, came together for a common purpose. Athletic space can also be interpreted as a kind of sanctuary, set apart from the everyday. One may likewise view the basketball courts or sports field in a turbulent neighborhood as an oasis—a place where interpersonal quarrels are suspended, enough at least to make the game possible. Although Olympic sport has lost its religious purpose, it can retain its status as sanctuary. Sport should mark a time and place where we deliberately put aside Hesiod's bad strife in order to engage the good strife of athletic competition.

The ancient Greeks' ability to compete peacefully, even with their enemies, may have roots even deeper than religion, in the venerable Hellenic tradition of *xenia* (hospitality). *Xenia* requires that Greeks welcome strangers and provide for their basic needs—even before knowing anything about them. It was a kind of unwritten pact among human beings, with obligations for the guest as well as the host, which was believed to be enforced by the same god to whom the Olympic Games were dedicated: Zeus. The tradition of *xenia* shows the importance of overcoming common human sentiments such as fear and hostility in the face of a stranger. Doing this effectively creates a space in which the roots of friendship can take hold.

It is a kind of interpersonal truce, the importance of which was not lost on modern thinkers such as Immanuel Kant, who declared "universal hospitality" to be the third article in his plan for perpetual peace among nations. No doubt aware of the ancient Hellenic tradition, Kant understood it to be guaranteed not by gods in the limited space of an Olympic festival but by the fact that all human beings share common ownership of the earth. The contemporary French philosopher Jacques Derrida affirms both the ancient and enlightenment conceptions of hospitality, identifying its importance not just with peace but with ethics. Says Derrida, "ethics is hospitality."

As a Panhellenic event attracting participants from a variety of city-states, the ancient Olympic festival took the religious, athletic, and cultural idea of sanctuary to an "international" level. The vehicle necessary for such a gathering was an official truce, known as *ekecheiria,* which allowed people from all over the Hellenic world to travel safely to Olympia. The Olympic truce did not, as is sometimes claimed, put an end to wars. Its main function was the protection of pilgrims traveling to and from the festival, but even this limited function makes it clear that the communal festival was regarded as *more important* than the worldly conflicts between city-states.

The truce shows that festival effectively trumped war, rendering the latter a baser activity (at least in the imagined opinion of the gods). In practice, the large and diverse gatherings at Olympia provided unparalleled opportunities for social and intellectual interaction. The religious dimension of the ancient Games helped to "enforce" the truce though it was not fail-safe. In 364 BCE, a battle took place within the sanctuary during the Games. But truce violations were notable for their rarity, and the effectiveness and duration of the ancient Games and their truce stand as an impressive demonstration of endurance in the eternal struggle for peace.

The modern Olympic truce is even more ambitious than the ancient one. Invoked with formal endorsement from the United Nations for all Games since 1993, the truce demands that nations follow the athletes' example and put aside their political differences at least for the duration of the Games. Although the modern truce usually falls short of its goal to stop conflicts worldwide, its successes are still remarkable. A ceasefire in Bosnia during the Lillehammer Games, for example, allowed an estimated 10,000 children to be vaccinated. More visibly, the Olympic teams of North and South Korea have marched together under one flag during various Opening Ceremonies.

Ultimately, the point of truce is to "open windows of opportunity for peace." Like the Olympic festival, and ideally sport itself, truce creates a time and place where conflicts are set aside, and a culture of peace has a chance to take root. Just as *xenia* required ancient Hellenes to make space and bring out their best for strangers, the Olympic Games cultivate peace by making a space in which to bring out our best as human beings.

Marble relief fragment depicting athletic prizes, 2nd century CE. The wreaths of sacred vegetation awarded to victors show the link between athletics and religion. Metropolitan Museum of Art number: 59.11.19.

Equality and Fair Play

The second lesson that Olympic sport can teach us about peace is that we must, on some level, recognize one another as equals. This principle too may derive from the religious origins of the Games since differences among human beings were regarded as insignificant in comparison with our collective inferiority to the gods. A more direct influence may have been the structure of sport itself, that is, the simple fact that athletic contests consider competitors to be equal under their rules.

Scholars have postulated that the function of athletic contests in the ancient Greek religious festival was to select a single "best" winner who would then be symbolically sacrificed to the god. The tokens of victory explicitly associate athletic victors with the animals used in ritual sacrifice. In order to perform such a scientific testing function, games must provide contestants with equal opportunity.

Such athletic equality stood in stark contrast to the highly stratified societies from which most ancient athletes hailed. Some scholars believe that athletic equality may even have influenced the development of democracy in ancient Greece. Noting that a free man was subject to the public punishment if he violated the rules of the contest, archaeologist Stephen G. Miller concludes that *isonomia,* or the concept of equality before the law, may be the greatest "creation" of ancient athletics.

In our modern world, where international law is already a fledgling reality, the idea that athletic games could be at the root of such a concept may seem strange. But it is hard to name another place where citizens from different communities governed by different laws get together and agree to be guided by one set of rules. Quite simply, sport is not possible unless competitors submit to a common set of rules, which defines them as equals. It is worth noting that at the time of the first modern Olympic Games (1896), there were no standardized international sports rules. Competitors in the triple jump, for example, used contrasting styles since the rules did not specify how the jump should be made.

It was in fact the establishment of the Olympic festival that spawned most international sports federations and the subsequent standardization of the rules. It may be objected that this standardization of rules amounts to nothing more than cultural hegemony, an agreement forced on competing parties by stronger authorities. Like the *pax romana,* this would be more the imposition of power than the cultivation of peace, but participation in athletic contests is by definition voluntary.

The fact is that athletic participation levels down social hierarchies. No matter the competitors' social or political status, the rules of the contest treat them as equal to one another and, in a sense, force them to treat each other as "equal under the law." The nudity of ancient athletes may be the most vivid illustration of this principle. As Miller puts it, "Once clothes are stripped off the human figure, it is difficult to distinguish the rich from the poor, the smart from the dumb, the aristocrat from the king or the democrat." Perhaps more significant in the social context of the ancient games, competitors faced the possibility of being flogged in public for rules violations. Since flogging was normally reserved for slaves, a free man's willingness to risk such shame is evidence of the atypical equality associated with Greek athletics.

The importance of equality under the law is reflected, among other places, in Immanuel Kant's 18th-century essay *Perpetual Peace.* Therein Kant proposes a civil contract among nations, akin to the traditional concept of a social contract, in which individuals give up just enough personal freedom to secure the much greater freedom provided by peace. This submission to common laws is viewed as completely voluntary because it is completely rational. Since the world itself is limited in terms of space, rational nations must secure their freedom by making agreements with others to live together in peace. The nation who refuses such an agreement must be either irrational or more interested in power than in peace. Plato's *Republic* argues likewise that peace in the city must be based on adherence to purely rational laws. Justice is identified with the harmonious function of individuals and communities, and injustice leads inevitably toward discord and civil war; it makes the community an enemy of itself.

Today's athletes may submit to the common rules of sport grudgingly, especially when there are personal or political differences, but they *must* enter the agreement in order to have the chance of victory. That drive for victory on a team level pushed the racial integration of sport and is currently pushing female participation—even where cultural obstacles exist. Says Olympic scholar Nikolaos Nissiotis, "sports transforms human aggressiveness—a biological, essential momentum which expresses the desire to dominate the other—into a means of sociable relations." Sport allows us to express our differences, maybe even anger, while still respecting our status as equals.

Perhaps even more important for the goal of peace, international contests such as the Olympic Games provide an educational spectacle in which the world sees diverse people treating each other as equals and voluntarily submitting to common rules. Indeed, Olympic competition illustrates the paradoxical ideal of competitive striving within a cooperative framework. So the second lesson about peace that the Olympic Games teach us is to treat one another as equals.

Solidarity and Mutual Understanding

The lesson of equality through sport creates a paradox. Aren't contests about finding winners? Aren't they designed to bring inequalities? Within this paradox lies the Olympic Games' third lesson about peace: we must learn to respect our differences. The roots of this lesson lie most probably in the nature of the ancient site itself. Although Olympia was dedicated primarily to Zeus, it hosted altars to a variety of gods and heroes. Furthermore, it was a Panhellenic site, serving not just a single city or region but the diverse panorama of peoples and cultures in the Ancient Greek world.

Every four years during the Games, the small valley space was packed with a huge variety of visitors. By coming to Olympia for common worship, feasting, and sport, this group created a new community—one more culturally and politically diverse than the communities from which they traveled. A modern might call this Olympic community "international," although the ancients had their own word: "cosmopolitan." In any case, Olympia and other Panhellenic festivals seem to have helped diverse groups tolerate their differences and identify themselves as commonly "Greek." It is likely that Olympic-style sport facilitated this unification.

Engaging in athletic competition with someone different in any number of ways helps not only to overcome stereotypes and confirm our common humanity but also, perhaps more importantly, to tolerate and even appreciate our differences. Imagine a pair of wrestlers, one Athenian and one Spartan, raised from birth to distrust each other. During the close-fought match, however, the stereotypes fade away because the sport requires them to respond to each other, not as Athenian or Spartan, but as wrestlers.

Ideally, they might come to appreciate their differences as wrestlers; perhaps one relies on strength and endurance, the other on speed and technique. As soon as they begin to evaluate one another in terms of their personal qualities, however, they begin to evaluate one another as people do *within* a single community. At this point, the Athenian and the Spartan have not lost their identities as Athenian and Spartan, nor has one absorbed the other into his culture; what has happened is that their idea of community has expanded to include persons and cultures that were previously excluded.

This intellectual community expansion reflects the ancient concept of cosmopolitanism or world citizenship. This idea bloomed when the Socratically inspired philosophy of Greek Stoicism faced the unprecedented racial and religious diversity of the Roman Empire. Both the Emperor Marcus Aurelius and the slave Epictetus embraced the essential unity of all mankind. Stoics viewed humanity as something like a single organism that depends for its health on the well-being of all its parts. The Stoic philosophers themselves hailed from every edge of the empire and must have found as much strength in their cultural diversity as philosophical agreement.

Stoic cosmopolitanism did not advocate withdrawal from particular communities (or even from participating in their communities' wars); rather, it posited a higher human community of which each individual is simultaneously a part. The sentiment is echoed by this description of Diogenes of Sinope (who is said to have coined the term "cosmopolis"):

> He would ridicule good birth and fame and all such distractions, calling them showy ornaments of vice. The only true commonwealth was, he said, that which is as wide as the universe. (Diogenes Laertius 2.7.19)

Stoic cosmopolitanism, like the Olympic founder Pierre de Coubertin's "sincere internationalism," did not depend on insulation from or imposition of one culture over another; rather, it sought to engage different cultures on some sort of common ground.

Athletic arenas are one such common ground, the valley of Olympia was another, eventually all of Hellas became a larger common ground, and by the time Kant wrote about international peace, the idea had expanded even farther. Allowing that nations may have particular borders and interests, Kant argued that all human beings nevertheless share common ownership of the earth. The globe itself is a kind of bordered community in which all human beings are entitled to certain basic rights, which Kant described as "cosmopolitan."

It may be daunting to imagine a world community, but the modern Olympic Games have been remarkably successful at presenting at least the image of one. Olympic sport continues to reveal commonalities while pointing out differences. Nissiotis describes the Olympic Games as "a world community beyond any kind of discrimination and hatred." The Olympics best illustrate their cosmopolitanism spirit when the athletes abandon national ranks and enter the closing ceremonies as one world made of many diverse individuals and groups. Olympic sport's third lesson about peace is that we can live with and even respect our differences.

Conclusion

Those who dream and write about ideal societies where peace prevails are frequently accused of uselessly building castles in the sky, but usually they are fully aware that the ideal is unrealizable. In his plea for peace, Erasmus laments the warring he finds ubiquitous among mankind—even among professors in the university and monks in the monastery. Saint Augustine is so frustrated by the problems of worldly conflict, he finally consigns true peace to the afterlife. And Kant ends *Perpetual Peace* with the declaration that making a just and peaceful world is a duty, "though only through an unending process of approximation to it." In philosophy, peace is always an ideal—but one worth striving for.

What is remarkable about the Olympics and peace is that the two came to be associated with one another at all. In this article I have suggested that the connection develops out of certain aspects of Olympic-style sport. Although the aspects derive from the particular cultural heritage of the Games, they still endure today. Olympic sport can teach us three lessons about peace: first, that we must deliberately set aside a time and place for it; second, that we must recognize others' equality; and third, that we must respect one another's differences within the larger world community.

Whatever the Olympic Movements political ambitions for international peace, the cultivation of harmony and concord among individuals in a community of any size should be recognized as a valuable and lasting gift contribution to the struggle. As Saint Augustine put it in *City of God* 19.12:

> Whoever reviews at all, with me, the pattern of human affairs and our common nature observes that just as there is no man who does not wish joy, so there is no man who does not wish peace.

Let the Olympic Games be more than an expression of this wish; let them be an instrument of peace—one that provides the opportunity for the peaceful values inherent in sport to offer their lessons to people who share this violent, cynical, and increasingly small world.

Bell-krater showing a torch-race among ephebes in a festival.
Attributed to the Kekrops Painter, ca. 400 BCE. Metropolitan
Museum of Art number 56.171.49. Open access image.

Glossary of Ancient Greek Terms

Agōn (ἀγών): denotes an assembly of spectators and contestants gathered for a competition, including sports, drama, and trials. The Olympics and other athletic festivals are referred to even in modern Greek as *agōnes* and not "games."

Aretē (ἀρετή): often translated "virtue," *aretē* is the quality that makes anything excellent in its kind. Sport was thought to reveal and celebrate human *aretē,* which showed our closeness to heroes and gods. In philosophy, *aretē* was a moral condition that enabled good action, similar to what we call "character."

Athla (ἄθλα), singular *athlos*: feats, contests, ordeals, labors as in those performed by Heracles (see also *ponoi*). An "athlete" is one who performs an *athlos*, not necessarily in sport.

Athlon (ἄθλον): the prize or reward the comes from an *athlos*, which is sometimes defined as a "contest for a prize," but the plural *athla*—especially in reference to the *athla* of Heracles—indicates his feats or labors, rather than their rewards. Prizes in ancient sport ranged from olive wreaths to money to songs.

Katharsis (κάθαρσις): a cleansing or purification that can be physical, spiritual, or mental—as in the clarification of ideas. It often results from *mimēsis,* as when our ideas about *aretē* are clarified by emulating heroic *athla* through sport.

Elenchos (ἔλεγχος): Socrates' method of questioning in order to examine or refute the beliefs of his interlocutors.

Ekecheiria (ἐκεχειρία): cessation of hostilities or truce. The ancient Olympic truce was originally a protection for pilgrims travelling to the festival; it did not stop wars.

Eudaimonia (εὐδαιμονία): usually translated "happiness," the term in Greek goes beyond subjective feeling to encompass objective criteria such as prosperity, good-fortune, social acceptance, and thriving.

115

Glossary

Kalokagathia (καλοκἀγαθία): a combination of beauty and goodness, the term used by Aristotle to describe a kind of super-*aretē* that makes good conduct effortless.

Kalon (καλόν): beauty or fairness, with moral as well as aesthetic connotations. The concept is usually applied to things as the adjective *kalos,* though *kallos* with two lambdas refers more specifically to physical beauty.

Kudos (κῦδος): the glory or renown brought about by heroic and athletic *athla,* sometimes thought to have a talismanic power for the recipient and their community.

Mimēsis (μίμησις): imitation, emulation, or representation, as when an actor represents a character or an athlete emulates the *athlos* of a hero in competition.

Parthenos (παρθένος): maiden, unmarried woman. *Parthenos* is the status between childhood and marriage, when females are sexually mature but still not married. Footraces were generally restricted to *parthenoi* or run by young girls before menarche as ritual preparation for becoming *parthenoi.*

Psychē (ψυχή): translated either as "mind" or "soul," *psychē* was understood as the feature of the human person that included their thoughts, emotions, and appetites.

Ponos (πόνος), plural *ponoi*: the kind of labor, effort, or toil required to achieve an athletic or heroic feat. Heracles' "labors" are called *ponoi* and Socrates uses that term to describe his philosophical "service" to the city of Athens in Plato's *Apology.*

Bibliography

The essays in this volume are based on papers published in scholarly journals. Footnotes, references, and citations have mostly been removed for ease of reading, but key primary and secondary sources are listed below along with suggested reading for those wishing to learn more about the Ancient Olympic Games and their philosophy.

Ancient Sources

Aelian. *Varia Historia*. Edited by Rudolf Hercher. Leipzig: Teubner, 1866.

Aristophanes. *Clouds*. Tr. Jeffrey Henderson. Cambridge, MA: Harvard University Press, 1998.

Aristotle. *The Complete Works of Aristotle*. Ed. Jonathan Barnes. 2 vols. Princeton, NJ: Princeton University Press, 1995.

Augustine. *City of God*. 7 vols. Tr. G.E. McCracken. Cambridge, MA: Harvard University Press, 1957.

Dio Chrysostom. *Discourses*. 2 vols. Tr. J.W. Cohoon. Cambridge, MA: Harvard University Press. 1939.

Diodorus Siculus. *Library of History*. Tr. C. H. Oldfather. Cambridge, MA: Harvard University Press, 1933.

Dionysius of Halicarnassus. *Roman Antiquities*. Tr. E. Cary. Cambridge, MA: Harvard University Press, 1943.

Hesiod. *Theogony. Works and Days. Testimonia*. Tr. G.W. Most. Cambridge, MA: Harvard University Press, 2018.

Homer, *Iliad*. Trans. Augustus T. Murray. Cambridge, MA: Harvard University Press, 1924.

Homer. *Odyssey*. Tr. Augustus T. Murray. Cambridge, MA: Harvard University Press, 1919.

Isidorus. *Etymologiae*. Tr. S.A. Barney et. al. Cambridge: Cambridge University Press, 2006.

Pausanias. *Description of Greece*. 5 vols. Tr. W.H.S. Jones. Cambridge, MA: Harvard University Press, 1918.

Philostratus. *Gymnasticus*. Tr. Jason König. Cambridge, MA: Harvard University Press, 2014.

Pindar. *Olympian Odes, Pythian Odes*. Tr. W. Race. Cambridge, MA: Harvard University Press, 1997.

Plato. *Complete Works*. Ed. John Cooper. Indianapolis, IN: Hackett, 1997.

Plutarch. *Lives*. Tr. Perrin Bernadotte. Cambridge: Harvard University Press, 1919.

Strabo. *Geography*. Ed. Horace L. Jones. Cambridge: MA: Harvard University Press, 1924.

Thucydides. *History of the Peloponnesian War*. Tr. Charles F. Smith. Boston: Ginn, 1913.

Xenophanes. *Fragments*. Tr. Douglas E. Gerber. Cambridge, MA: Harvard University Press, 1999.

Modern Sources

Briggs, R., H. McCarthy, and A. Zorbas. *16 Days: The Role of Olympic Truce in the Quest for Peace*. Athens: Demos, 2004.

Bourriot, Felix. *Kalos Kagathos-Kalokagathia: D'un terme de propaganda de sophistes à une notion sociale et philosophique: Etude d'histoire athenienne*. Spudasmata, 58. Hildesheim, Zurich, and New York: Georg Olms, 1995.

Calame, Claude. *Choruses of Young Women in Ancient Greece*. Tr. D. Collins and J. Orion. Lanham, MD: Rowman & Littlefield Publishers, 2001.

Crowther, Nigel. *Athletika: Studies on the Olympic Games and Greek Athletics*. Hildesheim: Weidemann, 2004.

Coubertin, Pierre de. *Olympism: Selected Writings*. Edited by Norbert Muller. Lausanne: International Olympic Committee, 2000.

Derrida, Jacques. *On Cosmopolitanism and Forgiveness*. London: Routledge, 2001.

Drees, Ludwig. *Olympia: Gods, Artists and Athletes*. New York: Praeger, 1968.

Erasmus. "The Complaint of Peace." In *The Essential Erasmus*. Tr. J.P. Dolan. New York: Mentor Books, 1963 (originally published in 1510), 174-204.

Finley, M.I., and Plecket, H.W. *The Olympic Games: The First Thousand Years*. New York: Viking, 1976.

Georgiadis, Konstantinos. *Olympic Revival: The Revival of the Olympic Games in Modern Times*. Athens: Ekdotike, 2003.

Golden, Mark. *Greek Sport and Social Status*. Austin: University of Texas Press, 2009.

Hawhee, Debra. *Bodily Arts: Rhetoric and Athletics in Ancient Greece*. Austin: University of Texas Press., 2004.

Hobbes, Thomas. *Leviathan*. Indianapolis, IN: Library of Liberal Arts, 1958 (originally published in 1651).

Kant, Immanuel. *Perpetual Peace and Other Essays*. Tr. T. Humphrey. Indianapolis, IN: Hackett, 1983 [1795].

Kurke, Leslie. *The Traffic in Praise: Pindar and the Poetics of Social Economy*. Ithaca: Cornell University Press, 1991

Lupu, Eran. *Greek Sacred Law: A Collection of New Documents*. Leiden: Brill, 2009.

Miller, Stephen G. *Ancient Greek Athletics*. New Haven, CT: Yale University Press, 2004.

Nagy, Gregory. *Ancient Greek Heroes, Athletes, Poetry*. New Alexandria Foundation, 2024.

Nagy, Gregory. *The Ancient Greek Hero in 24 Hours*. Cambridge, MA: Harvard University Press, 2013.

Nicholson, N.. *Aristocracy and Athletics in Archaic and Classical Greece*. Cambridge: Cambridge University Press, 2005.

Nissiotis, Nikolaos. "The Olympic Movement's Contribution to Peace." *Proceedings of the IOA* (1985): 54-63.

Papakonstantinou, Zinon. *Sport and Identity in Ancient Greece*. London: Routledge, 2019.

Raschke, Wendy, ed. *The Archaeology of the Olympics*. Madison: University of Wisconsin Press, 1988.

Roubineau, Jean-Manuel. *Milon de Crotone: ou l'"invention du sport*. Paris: Presses Universitaires de France, 2016.

Sansone, David. *Greek Athletics and the Genesis of Sport*. Berkeley: University of California Press, 1988.

Scanlon, Thomas F. *Eros and Greek Athletics*. New York: Oxford University Press, 2002.

Spivey, Nigel. *The Ancient Olympics*. Oxford: Oxford University Press, 2004.

Anthologies and Sourcebooks on Ancient Athletics:

Miller, Stephen G. *Arete: Greek Sports from Ancient Sources*. Berkeley: University of California Press, 2012.

Stocking, Charles and Susan Stephens. *Ancient Greek Athletics: Primary Sources in Translation*. Oxford: Oxford University Press, 2021.

Scanlon, Thomas F., ed. *Sport in the Greek and Roman Worlds* 2 vols. Oxford: Oxford University Press, 2014.

Also by Heather L. Reid

Reid, Heather. *Introduction to the Philosophy of Sport*. Lanham, MD: Rowman and Littlefield, 2012, 2nd ed. 2024.

Reid, Heather L. *Olympic Philosophy: The Ideas and Ideals behind the Ancient and Modern Olympic Games*. Sioux City, IA: Parnassos Press, 2020.

Reid, Heather L. *Athletics and Philosophy in the Ancient World: Contests of Virtue*. New York: Routledge, 2011.

Reid, Heather L. *The Philosophical Athlete*. Durham, NC: Carolina Academic Press, 2002, 2nd ed. 2019.

Reid, Heather. "Plato's Gymnastic Dialogues." In *Gymnastics, Athletics, and* Agōn *in Plato*, eds. H. Reid, M. Ralkowski, and C. Zoller. Sioux City: Parnassos Press, 2020. 15-30.

Reid, Heather L. "Performing Virtue: Athletic *Mimēsis* in Platonic Education." In *Politics and Performance in Western Greece*, eds. Heather L. Reid, Davide Tanasi, Susi Kimbell, Sioux City: Parnassos Press, 2017. 265-277.

Reid, Heather L. "Heroic *Parthenoi* and the Virtues of Independence: A Feminine Philosophical Perspective on the Origins of Women's Sport." *Sport, Ethics and Philosophy*, 14:3 (2020). 511-24.

www.ingramcontent.com/pod-product-compliance
Lightning Source LLC
Chambersburg PA
CBHW032137040426
42449CB00005B/279